The Art of the Atlantic Salmon Fly

PLATE I

The Return, by Henry McDaniel

THE ART OF THE

Atlantic Salmon

Fly

BY J. D. BATES

LINE DRAWINGS AND FRONTISPIECE

BY HENRY MCDANIEL

SWAN HILL

PRESS

OTHER BOOKS BY THE AUTHOR

Spinning for American Game Fish

Trout Waters and How to Fish Them

Streamer Fly Fishing in Fresh and Salt Water

Spinning for Fresh Water Game Fish

Spinning for Salt Water Game Fish

The Outdoor Cook's Bible

Streamer Fly Tying & Fishing
(with a subscribed limited edition of 600 copies)

Elementary Fishing

Atlantic Salmon Flies & Fishing
(with a subscribed limited edition of 600 copies)

Reading the Water

Fishing

How to Find Fish and Make Them Strike

The Atlantic Salmon Treasury (editor)

Streamers and Bucktails: The Big Fish Flies

Fishing
(revised, enlarged edition)

The Art of the Atlantic Salmon Fly

Copyright © 1987 Joseph D. Bates Jr.
Illustrations copyright © 1987 by Henry McDaniel.
Photograph plates II-XXIV copyright © 1987 by Werner Schmid.

First published in the United Kingdom in 1990
by Swan Hill Press, an imprint of
Airlife Publishing Ltd.
101 Longden Road, Shrewsbury SY3 9EB.

First published in the USA in 1989
by David R. Godine Publisher Inc.

ISBN 1-85310-154-0

Swan Hill Press

An imprint of Airlife Publishing Ltd.
101 Longden Road, Shrewsbury SY3 9EB, England

To my wife,
HELEN ELLIS BATES
in appreciation of fifty years of
understanding, cooperation
and affection

There is such a mute fascination in daintily dressed salmon flies, their outline so graceful, their tints so delicately blended and so cunningly contrasted, that no nature sensible of beauty can contemplate them with indifference.

SIR HERBERT MAXWELL, 1898

There is an indescribable *something* about a fly dressed by an expert amateur, who is a practical salmon fisherman, which the fly dressed by a non-angling professional not infrequently lacks. I have heard this peculiar quality rather neatly referred to as "Soul". A precise explanation of what is meant by "soul" is one of the impossibilities. The term is incomprehensible to the uninitiated, but is completely understood by the experienced man. Salmon fishing is full of these uncommunicable significances.

DR. THOMAS E. PRYCE—TANNATT, 1914

The classic British pattern has no peer. It is a bejeweled offering; it is an art form unto itself; it is a micro-history of far-flung anglers, worlds away from their rivers. It is for me a glimpse of that era when salmon fishing achieved its pinnacle of grace. It also catches salmon!

JOSEPH P. HUBERT, 1979

Contents

Introduction

HISTORIC changes mark the evolution of the Atlantic salmon fly. From unlikely trout and pike patterns produced as early as the fifteenth century, the palette shifts to simple and drab ones created exclusively for salmon, then to complicated examples of Victorian splendor, and finally back to the simpler patterns of more modern times. We trace this progression with emphasis on the elaborate Victorian "classics," marvelous gems of silks, tinsels, furs, and feathers. Although now not much used for fishing, the classics are being reborn as crowning challenges for fly tiers as well as fascinating treasures to collect, display, and own.

Even in earliest times salmon were noticed to rise to bits of flotsam and therefore were presumed to feed as trout do rather than rising virtually hungerless and presumably merely from instinct or curiosity. Thus, early salmon flies were trout patterns, augmented later by pike flies used for fish more amenable to the crude tackle in vogue then.

Early tackle consisted of a long and clumsy usually homemade rod with a plaited-horsehair line tied to its end. Old books imply that anglers avoided salmon because they could damage in seconds equipment requiring weeks to make. On hooking one, the angler often tossed his tackle in, letting the fish tow the floating rod until it tired. Then, with luck, the tackle and its prize could be regained.

With the midseventeenth-century development of the rod tip-top, reel, and running line, fly-fishing for salmon became more practical, but salmon patterns remained crude and meager until about a hundred years later. Then the salmon fly began to take on an appearance of its own.

Eighteenth-century flies used ingredients common to barnyard and glen. The birth of the gaudy and opulent classic patterns occurred in Ireland around 1800. These Irish flies were stylishly designed in vivid rainbow colors featuring crests and tippets of the golden pheasant and augmented by other gaudy embellishments. When examples of the colorful Irish patterns reached England they were denounced as "fish frights," even by anglers who acquired them through admiration. Fish frights or not, the Irish introductions did hook fish, especially when their brilliance was tempered by muted hues. For a time they coexisted with the duller patterns, which they gradually supplanted, evidently because anglers admired the gaudy flies more than the plain ones. They gave birth to the classic Atlantic salmon fly; the crowning gem of angling.

The classic salmon fly enjoyed growing popularity during the nineteenth century and into the beginning of the twentieth. While it was perhaps no more effective than its simpler counterparts, its bright colors and fancy ingredients appealed strongly to anglers. Fly tiers (fly *dressers* is the British term) were quick to foster this popular trend. They competed in developing increasingly glamorous and complex patterns, incorporating the rarest suitable feathers available.

If a prudent angler tried a new creation when salmon were on the take, his success validated the pattern, and it often became famous overnight. The fact that something else might have done as well or better wasn't often considered. All these different patterns finally comprised thousands—many thousands, if we include drab ones and variations. Some are still being fished by nostalgic anglers. While complex ones are in decline, the classic Atlantic salmon fly is enjoying lusty rebirth for other reasons.

Many people interested in angling are avid collectors of its accessories, including fishing flies. Increasing numbers specialize in the superior beauty of the Atlantic salmon classics. This obsession has also seduced the author, who has long been fascinated by the flies' ancient history, their intricate beauty, and the complexities of their construction.

I must admit, however, to a complete lack of interest in actually dressing the complicated classic patterns. I prefer to leave that demanding job to specialists. I tie flies very rarely, and then only to fish them, because there is always more satisfaction hooking salmon on flies we tie ourselves. As a fly tier, I am less than ordinary, though the salmon don't seem to realize this. As a student and collector, however, I have to admire the work of others.

This absorbing hobby began decades ago, prompted and developed by contacts with prominent historians, anglers, and fly dressers overseas. It resulted in acquisitions now numbering thousands. Some flies I own purely for fishing, some I have retained for sentiment, but most flies in my collection have been chosen because of rarity or excellence of construction. I soon learned that the best were not necessarily antiques or commercial European patterns. The handsomest and most precisely dressed patterns are most often tied by modern amateurs, many of whom have developed their craft into a fine art.

Until recently most of the usual classics have been British commercial efforts tied rapidly and often carelessly for maximum production and intended for fishing. To many Americans (and some others, of course) dressing these classics has become a challenge. Output is ignored. Time is forgotten. If it takes hours instead of minutes to do the job properly, that's accepted. It is the perfection of the fly itself that becomes essential; all other factors are insignificant. Results often are astounding to connoisseurs. For these flies are jewels of precision far too choice to ever suffer the rigors of a river—an observation which examinations of the patterns illustrated in this book will confirm.

It so happened that the publisher of this book, who also is a devoted salmon angler, viewed my collection and suggested a book based on it. Despite the many works treating salmon flies, none evidently has discussed their history from earliest times to the present, with emphasis on the beauty and complexity of most of the classic patterns. Hence the volume now in hand.

I have chosen not to include many antique flies, partly because their brilliance has dimmed with time, but mainly because, as previously noted, modern amateur fly dressers do superior work, and I believe their efforts should be recognized. I thank them for their contributions and only wish that many others, similarly gifted, could have been included.

One might question the propriety of modern patterns being included in a book about classics. It has been my intention to make this work as inclusive as possible, bringing it up to date by portraying examples of modern interest and thereby bringing the nearly 500-year-old history of fishing for Atlantic Salmon with flies to full circle.

J. D. BATES
Longmeadow, Massachusetts

List of Color Plates

List of Drawings and Photographs

Acknowledgments

THIS BOOK is the combined efforts of many people; principally the thirty-nine fly dressers who contributed patterns for the color plates and who are listed in the appendices. I thank each and every one most sincerely.

Their handiwork was expertly reproduced by Werner Schmid, an airline pilot who specializes in the photography of fishing flies and who also made the photographs on pages 93 and 221. My gratitude extends to him for his meticulous skill, and to Ronald Alcott, who ably assisted in mounting the more than three hundred examples for the twenty-three fly plates.

No book of this sort could succeed without an able artist who also is a salmon fisherman. My thanks go to Henry McDaniel for his black-and-white illustrations and for his kindness in contributing the use of one of his paintings for the frontispiece. It seemed proper for this to be a hen salmon on her way upstream, perhaps to be hooked and, ideally, properly released en route.

Henry McDaniel's title page illustration of "The Fairy Fly" was redrawn from that of the Reverend Henry Newland's book *The Erne, Its Legends and Its Fly Fishing* (London, 1851). The fly itself is similar to *Blacker's Number Ten* shown on Plate VI.

The drawing of the horse yacht on page 183 was made by Charles DeFeo, of New York City, and was previously included in *The Atlantic Salmon Treasury*.

Acknowledgment also is made to the Department of Rare Books of Princeton University, from which the six title-page photographs were purchased as well as the illustration on page 107.

The Art of the Atlantic Salmon Fly

CHAPTER ONE

Early Beginnings

THE STORY of the Atlantic salmon fly begins with the drab and subsequently evolves into the beautiful. The beautiful then diverges in part
to the more simplified modern patterns. But the fascination of this history to anglers, collectors, and fly dressers quite properly centers on the brilliant
and intricate patterns, largely of the nineteenth century, that are the focus of
this book. To understand them, however, we must start the story with their rather
colorless progenitors, flies which may make up in historical interest what they
may lack in esthetic allure.

If any interested readers are perplexed by this evolution, they might remind
themselves of the metamorphoses of insects, some of which are imitated for
fly-fishing. Two come to mind. The gorgeous butterfly or moth bursts from its
drab chrysalis. The prolific mayfly and its kin are born from the dull nymphs
which rise from stream beds to the surface, there to shuck their husks, spread
pulsating wings, and fly away.

Perhaps we can see in these insects' lives a similarity to the evolution of the
artificial salmon fly. It began before 1496, but that seems to be a good date to
start with because that year marks the publication of the first book about fly-
fishing. While little is said in it about salmon, the twelve flies described in the
book were basic to salmon-fly design for at least 250 years. In fact I am sure that
after 500 years or so, these ancient patterns would hook their share of salmon
today, but I have heard of no one ingenious enough to try it.

The famous book is *The Treatyse of Fysshynge wyth an Angle*, printed in 1496
by Wynkyn deWorde at Westminster, England, the first work on angling printed
in the English language. Wynkyn deWorde, incidentally, was the successor to

William Caxton (1422–1491), England's first printer, and the 1496 edition was done in Caxton's shop. It explains how rods, lines, and flies were made at that time and tells the best times of year to use the twelve fly patterns described. The book has been reprinted several times and is notably discussed in John McDonald's *Origins of Angling* (New York, 1947).

The Treatyse says its author was a Dame Julyana Bernes (later spelled Juliana Berners, or Barnes) and that she resided in the nunnery of Sopwell, near St. Albans. Tradition says she was beautiful and of noble birth. Dame Juliana describes how to make a two-piece fly rod from seasoned hazel, willow, or ash to which is attached a line of braided and tapered horsehair. She also explains how to fashion steel hooks from tempered, bent, and barbed needles for small fish and "greater hooks from larger needles" such as those used by embroiderers, tailors, or shoemakers. She tells how to affix hooks to lines and how to tie flies on the hooks. Such flies were intended mainly for fish such as trout and grayling, but Dame Juliana also mentions salmon.

Since reels and backing were unknown, and the line was looped directly to the rod tip, it is reasonable to assume that salmon were too formidable for even the sturdiest tackle of the day. Evidently salmon were hooked by accident. Why spend most of a winter fashioning fishing gear only to have a salmon damage or destroy it in seconds? The usual practice, if a salmon *were* hooked, was to toss the entire tackle into the river and let the fish tow the floating rod around until it was exhausted. Then, perhaps, the angler could wade out and retrieve the rod, possibly even landing his prize.

Our principal interest here is in the twelve flies the Treatyse describes, because, as has been said, they were the basis of patterns used (usually in larger sizes) for salmon for the next 250 years or so. These are reproduced in Plate II.

Since the Treatyse's dressing instructions were meager, it is natural for even the more erudite students to adapt them somewhat. The flies shown here were dressed by the eminent British expert Jack Heddon, of London. He has even interpreted them into modern parlance, complete with Latin names. I have compared these with interpretations by two great American experts, the before mentioned John McDonald and Dr. Dwight A. Webster, of Cornell University. These two gentlemen published an article in the May 27, 1957 issue of *Sports Illustrated* magazine that illustrated in color their conception of the twelve Treatyse flies as dressed by Dr. Webster. There is disagreement on how the flies should look, and this is certainly understandable considering the brevity of the

Here begynnyth the treatyse of fysshynge wyth an Angle.

Alamon in his parablys sayth that a good spyryte makyth a flouryng aege; that is a fayre aege & a longe. And syth it is soo: I aske this questyon. Whiche ben the meanes & the causes that enduce a man in to a mery spyryte.: Truly to my beste dyscrecyon it semeth good dysportes & honest gamys in whom a man Ioyeth wythout ony repentannce after. Thenne folowyth it þ gode dysportes & honest games ben cause of mannys fayr aege & longe life. And therfore now woll I chose of foure good dysportes & honeste gamys that is to wyte: of huntynge: hawkynge: fysshynge: & foulynge. The beste to my symple dyscrecyon whyche is fysshynge : callyd Anglynge wyth a rodde : and a lyne

Frontispiece to the original edition of the *The Treatyse of Fysshynge wyth an Angle* (1496)

descriptions in the Treatyse. Starting at the top left of Plate II these flies, as originally given, are:

FOR MARCH (1 and 2)

The dun fly: The body of dun wool and wings from the partridge.

Another dun fly: The body of black wool and wings from the blackest drake, with the feathers of the jay under the wing and under the tail.

FOR APRIL (3)

The stone fly: The body of black wool, with yellow under the wing and under the tail and the wings of the drake.

FOR MAY (4, 5, and 6)

The ruddy fly: In the beginning of May a good fly is made with ruddy (red) wool for the body, wound about with black silk and with wings (sections of flight feathers) of the drake and of red capon's hackle.

The yellow fly: The body of yellow wool; the wings of red cock's hackle and of the drake, dyed yellow.

The black leaper (moth): The body of black wool, wound about with the herl of the peacock's tail, and the wings of the red capon, with a blue head.

FOR JUNE (7, 8, and 9)

The dun cut: The body of black wool with a yellow stripe at either side, and the wings of the buzzard bound with barked hemp.

The maure (moor) fly: The body of dark wool and the wings of the blackest male of the wild drake.

The tandy fly: The body of tawny wool and the wings back to back made from the whitest outer feathers of the male wild drake.

FOR JULY (10 and 11)

The wasp fly: The body of black wool, wound about with yellow thread, and wings of the buzzard.

The shell fly: The body of green wool, wound about with herl from the peacock's tail, and wings of the buzzard.

FOR AUGUST (12)

The drake fly: The body of black wool, wound about with black silk, and wings of the male black drake, with a black head.

Drab and crude as they may be, these Treatyse flies must begin any discussion of the salmon flies' evolution. They are the bedrock of all that follows, and their influence reaches into the present day. Dressed up a little, they obviously influence later dressings such as the midnineteenth-century Tweed patterns shown in Plate IV. My own fly books contain modern similarities such as *Black Heron, Black Fairy, Sweep,* and *March Brown.* Some of these, roughed up by salmon, closely resemble the Treatyse patterns.

Dame Juliana's Treatyse is fact adulterated with fiction. It evidently is a compilation of several even older manuscripts.* There were probably at least a dozen fourteenth- and fifteenth-century Middle English manuscripts covering the same ground and predating the Treatyse.

The fiction is that, so far as is known, there never was a Dame Juliana Berners, beautiful, noble, or otherwise. It seems that printer Wynkyn deWorde dreamed her up because he needed an author's name for the manuscript. Her genealogy and other "facts" about her were fantasies of later writers. The twelve ancient flies, however, are solidly embedded in angling history.

The sixteenth century showed only scant improvement in tackle, tactics, and flies. The latter principally were the Treatyse patterns or minor variations. Sport fishing for salmon was uncommon, due principally to inadequacy of tackle. In 1614 an unscrupulous author named Gervaise Markham published a book called *The English Husbandman.* Markham was a plagiarist who would be ignored today except for notes added by his editor, expert angler William Lawson. These notes include the first mention of *fly casting* in the English language, as well as the first allusion to the use of cork to make flies float "folded so cunningly about the hook that nothing may be perceived but the point and beard onely."

Lawson also says that artificial flies are to be moved upon the waters and then "will be taken greedily"; evidently the first mention of *fishing the fly.* He publishes a drawing of a fly which resembles a house fly on a hook.

"Dapping" was another popular method of fishing the fly at the time; that is, letting a fly on a light line blow with the breeze so it dances on the water. A fly suited for this purpose might have resembled the *Tandy Fly,* described in the Treatyse and illustrated in Plate II.

In 1651 Thomas Barker, a famous cook and angler who modestly said he was "not a scholar," wrote a small book of forty pages titled *Barker's Delight, or The*

---

* See "A New Treatise on the Treatyse" by Professor Richard C. Hoffman in *The American Fly Fisher,* Volume 4, Number 3, Summer 1982.

Art of Angling. In it is found a section on salmon fishing, the first authentic mention of a *reel* and *running line*, a vague description of an artificial fly intended purely for salmon, information on "dubbing" (hairs such as seal's fur or wool applied for a fly's body), and the first mention of *wound hackles* in English angling literature.

In Barker's 1657 edition he mentions and crudely illustrates what he calls a "winder," used by him for adjusting line length when trolling for pike. Two years earlier Izaak Walton, in his 1655 edition, mentions the use of a "winch" for salmon fishing. As Walton evidently had no direct experience in salmon fishing, he must have obtained his information from an earlier source, as Barker probably did.

Here's what Barker says about salmon angling:

> I will now shew you the way to take a salmon. The first thing you must gain must be a rod of some ten foot in the stock, that will carry a top of six foot pretty stiffe and strong, the reason is, because there must be a little wire ring at the upper end of the top for the line to run through, that you may take up and loose the line at your pleasure; you must have your winder within two foot of the bottom to goe on your rod made in this manner, with a spring, that you may put it in as low as you please. [In other words the *reel*, or "winder," as it was known, was attached to the butt by a spring clip in a position that could be altered according to preference. Barker goes on to say:]
>
> The salmon swimmeth most commonly in the midst of the river . . . if you angle for him with a flie (which he will rise to like a Trout) the flie must be made of a large hook, which must carry six wings, or four at least; there is judgement in making those flies. . . . You must be sure that you have your line of twenty-six yards in length that you may have your convenient time to turn him: but if you turn him you are very like to have the fish with small tackles: the danger is all in the running out both of Salmon and Trout, you must forecast to turn the fish as you do a wild horse, either upon the right or left hand and wind up in your line as you finde occasion in the guiding the fish to the shore, having a good large landing hook (a gaff) to take him up.

So here, 165 years after the publication of the Treatyse, we see real progress! We have a rod with a tip-top and a reel holding a longer line. We have a fly for salmon which has two or three pairs of wings and, since there is "judgement" to be used in tying it, evidently it can be dressed in various color combinations such as the one at the top of Plate III. About fifty years later, in his book *The Angler's Sure Guide* (1706) R. H., Esquire (attributed to Robert Howlett) mentions "loops," or line guides, later called "*guide-rings*," being added to rods.

During the seventeenth and early eighteenth centuries salmon flies of various colors with four or six wings (two or three pairs) seem usual. R. (Richard) Brookes, M. D. in his *The Art of Angling* (1766) makes this a little clearer:

> There is a Fly called the Horse-leech fly, which he (the salmon) is very fond of; they are of various Colours, have great Heads, large Bodies, very long Tails, and two, some have three, Pair of Wings, placed behind each other. Behind each Pair of Wings whip the Body about with Gold or Silver Twist, or both, and do the same by the Head. . . .

Dr. Brookes calls this pattern the *Horse-leech*, and it seems nearly the same as Barker's version of about a hundred years earlier. Both seem to imitate the dragonfly, but why it was assumed that salmon would be interested in them is a question upon which we can only conjecture. The answer may be that the immature forms of the various species of the dragonfly (order Odonata) are aquatic. For whatever reasons, imitations of dragonflies, crude as they were, were very popular in early times. In addition to being called "dragon flies" they also were known as "pike flies" and "salmon flies," which reminds us that some of these early patterns originally were intended for pike. A descendant of them is the long-bodied *Erin-Go-Bragh* illustrated on Plate VII.

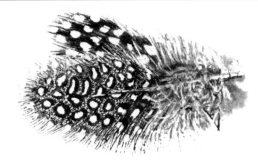

CHAPTER TWO

Glimmerings of Color

W ITH TACKLE developed to the point where anglers could reasonably hope to succeed with the King of Fishes, we encounter a very accomplished fly-rodder in the person of Captain Richard Franck. Here was an adventurer who fished for salmon in Scotland, visited North America, and wrote *Northern Memoirs* in 1658, a book finally published thirty-six years later in 1694.

Franck was an officer serving under the Lord Protector, Oliver Cromwell (1599–1658). His book is turgid, pedantic, and verbose. For me, its principal bright spot is that Franck carried a "dubbing bag," that is, a fly-tying kit, so he could dress flies on location to take advantage of his evaluation of fishing conditions.

Since the contents of Franck's dubbing bag show progress over the previously drab fly-tying materials, which usually were confined to products of farm, moor, or glen, let's hear what was in it:

> If salmon or trout be your recreation, remember always to carry your dubbing bag about you, wherein there ought to be silks of all sorts, threads, thrums [waste pieces of yarn], moccado-ends, and cruels of all sizes, and variety of colours; diversified and stained wool, with dogs and bears hair; besides twisted fine threads of gold and silver; with feathers from the capon, partridg, pheasant, mallard, smith [merganser], teal, snite [snipe], parrot, heronshaw, paraketta, bittern, hobby [falcon], phlimingo, or Indian flush [scarlet ibis]; but the mockaw, without exception, gives flames of life to the hackle.

Here, nearly 150 years before color finally blossomed out in fly dressing, we find an angler who used gold and silver threads (probably for ribbing), pheasant

Northern Memoirs,

Calculated for the

Meridian of SCOTLAND.

Wherein moſt or all of the **Cities, Citadels, Sea-ports, Caſtles, Forts, Fortreſſes, Rivers and Rivulets** are compendiouſly deſcribed.

Together with choice Collections of Various Diſcoveries, Remarkable Obſervations, Theological Notions, Political Axioms, National Intrigues, Polemick Inferences, Contemplations, Speculations, and ſeveral curious and induſtrious Inſpections, lineally drawn from Antiquaries, and other noted and intelligible Perſons of Honour and Emineney.

To which is added,

The Contemplative & Practical Angler, by way of Diverſion. With a Narrative of that dextrous and myſterious Art experimented in *England*, and perfected in more remote and ſolitary Parts of *Scotland*.

By way of Dialogue.

Writ in the Year 1658, but not till now made publick,

By **Richard Franck**, Philanthropus.

Plures necat Gula quam Gladius.

LONDON,
Printed for the Author. To be ſold by *Henry Mortclock* at the *Phenix,* in St. *Paul's* Church-yard. 1694.

Title page of Franck's *Northern Memoirs* (1694)

feathers (golden pheasant?), red, green, yellow, and blue feathers of parrot or macaw, pink of flamingo and scarlet ibis, and the lovely muted colors of parakeets!

We wish Franck had described some of the flies he dressed with these colorful ingredients, but he tells us nothing. What a loss! It is of interest that he mentions dogs' and bears' hair. Was this for hair-wings? He doesn't say clearly, but if they were, hair-winged flies are more ancient than we have supposed. He also doesn't mention such standard ingredients as feathers from turkeys, swans, geese, ducks, and even chickens.

Evidently Franck's flies were improvisations fashioned to suit conditions. He says, "For the brighter the day is, the obscurer your fly; but the more promiscuous the season is, by so much the more ought your fly to be bright and shining."

Around Franck's time other authors described contemporary tackle and flies. The double hook, for example, preferred by about half modern fly-fishermen and more or less spurned by the rest, is often considered a recent development. It was mentioned as long ago as 1590 in Leonard Mascall's *A Book of Fishing with Hooke & Line*, however, and it also is discussed by Colonel Robert Venables in his *The Experienced Angler* (1662) wherein we also find comments on salmon flies and the first mention of *upstream fishing*.

Venables was one of three Cromwellian soldiers (including Franck and Barker) who were also anglers and angling authors. His little book of about 100 pages was included in the fifth edition of Izaak Walton's *The Universal Angler* (1676), and it was printed separately in 1662 and in later editions. Here's what he says about double hooks:

> Young salmons . . . have tender mouths, so as they are apt to break their hold; to obviate which inconvenience, I have known some that use to fasten two hooks together . . . not with the points opposite to one another, but about a quarter of a Circle from each other, and on them they make their Flie, that if one Hook break hold, the other may not fail.

The method consisted of filing two similar hooks on opposite sides of each of the two shanks to make flat surfaces which could be set together so the bends and barbs would tilt from each other at an angle of about 45 degrees or more. The two hooks were tightly wrapped with tying thread to hold them as securely as possible in position. Since they were hinged by the flat sides of the two shanks, the bends and barbs could be carried closed and could be opened to the double-hook angle by pressing them apart with the thumb.

Venables printed his comments in 1662. Compare them with modern opinion. He says you must keep the fly in continual motion and that larger flies should be used in high or muddy water and smaller ones when it is clear. He recommends a red or orange fly for brownish water and a dark one for dark weather. He says that for every sort of fly we should have light, medium, and dark varieties to suit all water and weather conditions. While he was the first author to mention upstream fishing, the method didn't become firmly established until nearly two centuries later.

Still, up to the middle of the eighteenth century, and even from then on, although to a rapidly declining extent, artificial flies for salmon were the old Treatyse patterns or adaptations of them. In 1747 (the year given it in the catalogue of the Bodleian Library) Richard Bowlker published *The Art of Angling*, which rejected the Treatyse patterns as being "seldom useful to fish with." Bowlker gives a list of twenty-nine more or less new patterns, of which two are recommended particularly for salmon. He says that "salmon, being fond of anything that is gaudy, will rise to almost any of the trout flies when salmon are plenty."

The second and later editions of Bowlker's work were published by his son, Charles, who augmented them somewhat. He provides patterns which included the "monstrous" *Horse-leech*, and describes the second and third dressings designed exclusively for salmon so far found in angling literature.

The first of these was called the *Dragon Fly*, also named *Libella*, or *Libellula*.

> The wings are made of a reddish brown feather from the wing of a cock turkey, the body of auburn-coloured mohair warped with yellow silk, and ginger cock's hackle wrapped under the wings. Or it may be varied thus: the wings of a rich brown feather from a heron's wing; the body drab, or olive-coloured mohair, a bittern's hackle under the wings, and a forked tail. This fly is about two inches in length.

A fly of similar description would hook salmon today, some 200 years after this pattern was originated, and it could have either a hair or a feather wing. Our popular *Red Abbey* comes to mind, with silver tinsel ribbing instead of yellow silk.

The second of this ancient triumvirate is the historic *King's Fisher*, sometimes called the *Peacock Fly*. Charles Bowlker says about it,

> This is also a Salmon fly, and it is seen at the same time as the Dragon Fly. The wings are made of a feather from the neck or tail of a peacock; the body of deep green mohair, warped with light green silk; and a jay's feather striped blue and white, wrapped under the wings. It may be thus varied: the wings of a dark shining green feather from a drake's wing; the body of green mohair warped with chocolate silk, and a bittern's hackle under the wings.

THE
Art of ANGLING

Improved, in all its parts, Especially

FLY-FISHING:

CONTAINING

A particular Account of the several Sorts of Fresh-Water FISH, with their most proper BAITS.

ALSO

The Names, Colours, and Seasons of all the most Useful FLIES.

With Directions for making each FLY Artificially In the most Exact manner, &c.

The whole Interspers'd with many Curious and Uncommon Observations.

BY
RICHARD BOWLKER.

Et piscem tremula Salientem ducere Seta. Mart:

WORCESTER:
Printed by *M. Olivers*, in *High-Street.*

1748

Title page of Bowlker's *The Art of Angling* (1747)

These flies are reproduced on Plate III, with two versions of the *Peacock Fly*. We note that a feather from the tail of a peacock necessarily must be a large one, but it might pulsate enough in fast water to make it successful. Evidently the smaller neck feathers were popular. In Bowlker's 1780 edition he says, "He is called the King's Fisher from the beautifulness of his colour; but the Peacock Fly I think the most proper name, being so near the colour of the feathers that grow upon the *neck* of a peacock, as this fly's wings and body are." Evidently, strips of peacock tail or sword were also used, as one of the flies on Plate III illustrates.

Eric Taverner in his excellent book *Fly Tying for Salmon* (London, 1942) gives a pattern said to have been dressed in 1775 which was lent to him by Messrs. Allcock & Company. His inspection of it provides the following dressing, an interpretation of which is shown on Plate III:

Tag	Two turns of medium-width silver tinsel, flat		red and also undyed. The body tapering to the shoulder, where it is picked out
Tail	Some strands of wing material	*Throat*	Very dark blue dun cock
Body	Mixed pig's wool and mohair, dyed orange and red, blood-	*Wing*	Peacock tail-covert
		Head	Bronze peacock herl

The hook of this fly has a slightly compressed bend, more oval than rounded. This seems to be the first example of a fly with a metal tag, although Captain Franck and his associates might have used metal tags over a hundred years earlier, for the Captain mentions "twisted fine threads of gold and silver" as having been among the contents of his dubbing bag. We don't know, but since they were "twisted" instead of being flat, they probably were confined to ribbing.

One more pattern should suffice to indicate salmon-fly style in the late 1700s. It is found, without a name, in *The North Country Angler* (1786) and a reproduction of it is included in Plate III:

Tail	Five or six strains of a peacock's feather	half the size of the other and to lie flat on the hook; the
Body	Peacock herl	upper pair of dark mottled
Hackle	Black cock, three or four feathers, taken up the body	drake or turkey tail; dubbing between the wings of bright-
Wing	Double, the under pair only	brown pig's wool

Head A little yellow (pig's) wool mixed with brown

Eyes Beads sometimes are added for these

Hook Long-shanked

This double-winged fly undoubtedly reverts to the previously discussed *Horse-leech* described by Barker (1657) and by Chetham (1681); a sort of dragonfly. Small beads sometimes were used to represent eyes on the "great heads" of such patterns, and they were dressed on "large," or long-shanked, hooks. Thus the peculiar notion that salmon commonly struck at dragonflies or their representations existed for over a hundred years.

By now salmon flies (on eyeless, or blind, hooks) usually were tied directly to lengths of silkworm gut rather than horsehair, the other end being looped and joined to the loop of the "reel-line" so flies could be easily detached and others substituted. The close of the eighteenth century also saw the introduction of the *vise* into fly dressing. This is described in Samuel Taylor's *Angling in All its Branches* (1800).

The beginning of the nineteenth century saw salmon-fly design become more stabilized and, here and there, more colorful. An early example is found in *The Fly Fisher's Guide* (1816) by a knowledgeable angler named George C. Bainbridge. Bainbridge was the first author to mention the use of *hackle pliers* and of the *whip-finish knot* for securing thread in finishing a fly. His was the first angling book to contain color plates and the first one to show a color plate of salmon flies. The five illustrated are reproduced on Plate III.

We are most interested in Bainbridge's *Gaudy Fly* because it is perhaps the best known of early English colorful patterns. Bainbridge said it would "frequently raise fish when all the imitations of nature have proved unsuccessful." Its high and full wing is in the style of standard patterns popular much later. Here is Bainbridge's dressing of it:

> The wings, the extreme end of the feather of a guinea-fowl, not stripped, but having the feather left on both sides of the middle stem; a blood red hackle should be fastened on with the wings, and so arranged as to extend beyond them. The dyed feathers used by officers in the army answer very well for this purpose if those from the macaw can not be procured. The body is best made from the harl of an ostrich, dyed to correspond with the red feather introduced, with a bright yellow hackle over it. The beautiful green feather, which forms

the eye of the peacock's tail, should be fastened at the head, and left hanging downwards, so as to cover the body for nearly half an inch; and a few strips of the same part of the feather may be fastened at the tail.

Bainbridge's other four flies can be mentioned briefly. The *Spring Fly* and the *Summer Fly* are recommended for those times of year. The *Summer Fly*, with its long body, reminds us of dragonfly types previously mentioned. The *Quaker Fly* is so named because of its drabness; a characteristic we currently prefer to avoid. The *Wasp Fly*, supposedly imitating a wasp, was made with a yellow wool body and black hackle, or vice versa. So what's so new about the modern *Woolly Worm*?

George A. Hansard, in his *Trout & Salmon Fishing in Wales* (1834) says that the above five patterns long remained standard on northern Welsh rivers. "The flies ordinarily used by the Welsh native anglers are very sober in colour, and few in number." The *Gaudy Fly* is called *Ogmore* by Hansard because it was very popular in the area in Wales of the river of that name.

It seems important to note here that, by the beginning of the nineteenth century, the preponderance of English, Scotch, and Welsh salmon flies had settled into a type exemplified by Bainbridge's and Hansard's *Spring* and *Quaker* flies. This evolved into a more or less standard character, or peculiarity of shape and general construction, popular to this very day. Examples are the early Tweed patterns illustrated on Plate IV. This characteristic also was developed in Irish patterns, but they were much gaudier and more brilliant, as we soon shall see.

Why did these characteristics develop? Evidently they occurred by trial and error or physical evolution, salmon flies having descended from insect-imitating trout patterns. Obviously the salmon must have approved, or this evolution would have proceeded differently. Why did the salmon prefer a simulated "fly," a dragonfly, moth, or butterfly? They didn't find them at sea, and their memory of them from the time when the salmon were parr or smolts would be remote. On their return to their native rivers, while nature stifles their hunger, they do sample tidbits occasionally, however, and perhaps because of conditioned reflex, salmon instinctively react to the motion of small, moving objects that might be a variety of prey. The correctly dressed salmon fly has a pulsating wing and hackles, which give a rhythmic action that incites strikes. This peculiarity of shape and motion seems to trigger this reflex. All that remains is to make the fly visible to the fish, in the correct size and colors for various conditions. The often quoted similarity of the classic salmon fly shape to that of butterflies or moths seems largely to be an inherited coincidence, but it was grasped by fly dressers because it could be developed into beautiful patterns inspired by the insects themselves.

Before going on to more brilliant and gaudier temptations, let's look at the general characteristics of the relatively drab patterns exemplified by those used on the River Tweed in the early 1800s. They were drab because they were made from handy materials readily available in barnyards and by hunting. More exotic materials must have been available, but evidently fly dressers didn't realize their potentialities at the time.

To explore the patterns associated with this celebrated stream, let's go Tweed-side in Scotland to meet a doughty shoemaker who put aside his tools as often as possible in favor of his fly rod. He is John Younger, who wrote *River Angling* in 1840, a book republished in a second edition in 1860 when the author was seventy-five years old.

Younger claims origination of six patterns illustrated on Plate IV. One of these, which he calls *Second Fly*, is most surely his version of the famous *Toppy* described by John Kirkbride in his book *The Northern Angler* (1837) and discussed in many books since then, including William Scrope's *Days and Nights of Salmon Fishing on the Tweed* (1843). Kirkbride says of it,

> In the Tweed, a black turkey feather, tipt with white, kills remarkably well. Let the tail be of yellow mohair, with a tip of silver; make the body of black mohair, or worsted, rib it with gold twist, and hackle it with a black-listed red feather from the neck of the gamecock; put a little orange pig's wool, or mohair, at the shoulders; let the wings be of a black turkey feather, with a small tip of white.

Scrope's six patterns, which Younger says he purloined from him but which appear rather different from Younger's, are also shown on Plate IV. These are typical of early Tweed flies and of other rivers at the time which were not influenced by Irish brilliance.

Younger says that the brilliant Irish patterns were introduced into Scotland in 1810. On most rivers they were greeted with derision and dismissed as wanton fripperies. Less extreme anglers favored them when bright flies were considered necessary or incorporated some parts of their elegance into the relatively somber dressings they preferred.

Following the earliest introduction of colorful flies from Ireland, some progress toward brilliance was made by Belton's book *The Angler in Ireland* (1834) but, in general, patterns everywhere in the United Kingdom except the Emerald Isle were on the drab side until just before midcentury. Then, for reasons we shall soon examine, they blossomed out into a piscatorial burst of brilliance.

CHAPTER THREE

Birth of Brilliance

W'E'LL NEVER KNOW why Pat McKay happened to visit the Ballyshannon millinery shop near the River Erne in northwestern Ireland early in the nineteenth century, but the fact that he did influenced the transformation of salmon flies from drab to gaudy and all hues in between. We do know that Pat was the innovative shining light of a well-known fly-tying family, and we know about some of the gorgeous flies he originated, but little else is known of his life. Even the dates of his birth and death are unknown.

In rural Ireland most people were illiterate, so most angling information was transmitted verbally, a process that doubtless distorted some facts. Pat McKay evidently lived and dressed salmon flies between about 1810 and 1870, but other information about him, except for his salmon-fly patterns, is conjecture.

He must have been amazed at what he found in that Irish shop: silk threads and flosses of every color; skins of the golden pheasant, and cock-of-the-rock, blue chatterer, Indian crow, parrot, macaw, and other exotic feathers from South America and other far-flung parts of the world. This was the heyday of British world trade, and unusual imports were common. While Ballyshannon was not a noted seaport, the profusion of salmon in the River Erne made it a mecca for anglers, and therefore a center of fly dressers. The noted Rogan family lived near the bridge at Ballyshannon. Competition among fly dressers was intense.

Pat evidently considered that innovative patterns might increase sales and that brilliant varieties would appeal more than the usual drab designs. The artist in him was tempted to experiment with smooth silk flosses for bodies instead of rougher seals' fur or pigs' wool. The golden crest feathers (toppings) and black-banded orange breast feathers (tippets) of the golden pheasant especially caught his eye.

What might the salmon think of such gaudy designs? Pat knew that fresh-run fish savored almost anything; even bits of bread or small coins dropped from a bridge would get attention. Experimentation indicated that bright flies could be seen better than drab ones in discolored water. He was also confident that anglers would buy the colorful flies, and that they would prefer them to duller patterns. Pride of possession existed even then!

Armed with his new purchases from the milliner, Pat returned to his cottage to experiment. We don't know how many attempts he made or how long he took, but we do know that the fruit of his labor was a fly pattern that started a trend that never stopped—the progenitor of the famous Parson Series, as illustrated on Plate V, the lovely

Golden Butterfly

Tag Fine silver twist and gold floss silk

Tail A golden pheasant topping and barred wood duck

Butt Black ostrich herl

Body Yellow floss silk

Ribbing Medium gold twist

Throat Three toppings, curved *downward*

Wing A topping applied *edgewise* on each side of the body to curve inward, both ends meeting midway along the tail; also one large topping tied on top to curve *upward*

Cheeks A cock-of-the-rock feather on each side tied high and edge-wise, and a kingfisher feather on each side tied low

Head Black ostrich herl and black tapered thread, varnished

Fly dressers and historians may wish to make special note of this unusual pattern. Reverend Henry Newland in his book *The Erne: Its Legends and Its Fly Fishing* (1851) says the first Parson was originated in 1836, but since this fly is considered the progenitor of the Parson Series, it must have evolved before that date, though it seems impossible to know how long before. John Younger in his *River Angling* (1840) says that Irish flies "made like butterflies, of parrot, golden pheasant and other bright fancy feathers" were known in Scotland "within thirty years back," which would be about 1810. So-called "gaudy" flies evolved gradually but blossomed out early in the nineteenth century. While the *Golden Butterfly* wasn't the first one, it is one for which we have a definite pattern, and it is surely the most famous.

Note the unusual wing. Looking down at it when its hook's curve is downward, the two toppings, applied edgewise beside the body, curve to resemble the gunwales of a boat. The third topping is applied in reverse, to curve upward rather than downward. The three toppings of the throat also are the reverse of normal application. Perhaps the reason is that this arrangement provided greater mobility in the water. We will soon see that James Rogan and his son, Michael, also adopted reversed toppings in wings. The idea didn't seem to catch on, but it was popular for a time on the Erne and is seen in three of the six patterns illustrated in Reverend Newland's book.

Pat McKay seems to have been a promoter of brilliant patterns. He tied flies for famous people and probably guided them as well. He tied them for O'Gorman, author of *The Practice of Angling* (1845), for Dr. Shiel, Lord Bolingbroke, and their friends, and later for Francis Francis, author of *A Book on Angling* (1867). While many excellent fly dressers were working throughout Ireland, Pat McKay seems the most noteworthy.

For many years around 1836, when the first Parson pattern was originated, the four fishable miles of the Erne were owned by a gentleman named Dr. S. Shiel. Dr. Shiel was very liberal with his pools, the fishing of which is entertainingly described by the Reverend Newland. Pat McKay dressed flies for Dr. Shiel, who gave them to many of his guests. One such pattern was the original:

Parson No. 1

MCKAY'S ORIGINAL PATTERN

Tag	Fine silver twist and orange floss
Tail	A topping
Body	Yellow silk floss
Ribbing	Fine silver tinsel, closely wound
Body hackle	Lemon yellow, wound palmer-style
Throat hackle	Golden yellow, tied full
Wing	Two tippet feathers, back to back, with three red-tipped toppings curved over to meet point of tail. The wing is as wide as possible
Side cheeks	Cock-of-the-rock tied butterfly-style, i.e., sticking out at the sides like a fan
Head	Golden yellow pig's wool and black thread

Concerning *Parson No. 1* we have a difference in historical opinion, as given in an undated letter from Dr. Shiel to Francis Francis and published by him:

MY DEAR SIR: I send four Parsons I have borrowed from Mr. Hobson, and will send you a couple made with summer duck (wood duck) in the wing. The first Parson, and called from him, was used by the Rev. Arthur Meyrick, of Romsbury; it was two large toppings, a yellow body, yellow hackle, very thin twist run close altogether up the body—I mean half as close as in any of those flies I send. He said he got it from Lord Bolingbroke at Christchurch. He changed the body to orange; both were silk bodies.

The late Mr. William Larket, of Derby, put cock-of-the-rock in the wing. I think I put the first fur body to the fly—it was orange pig's wool. Mr. Larket and then Mr. Hobson added to this the purple and fiery brown under the wing, which Pat McKay borrowed and adopted, and nothing has beaten this pattern.

YOURS,
S. SHIEL

Dr. Shiel didn't mention tippets in the wing. No Parson would have a wing of only two (or three) toppings. Authorities in Ireland give credit to Pat McKay, rather than to Mr. Larket, for adding the splayed cock-of-the-rock. We see here what so often occurs to famous patterns. Variations multiply, sometimes because the correct ingredients aren't available, but more often because reproducers like to introduce their own ideas. The original patterns mentioned in this chapter, and a few of the more important variations, are illustrated in Plate V.

Those flies resulted particularly in a pattern which has been altered a bit by later authors, the gorgeous *Golden Parson* correctly given in Francis, as follows:

Golden Parson

FRANCIS FRANCIS' PATTERN

Head Black

Tag Silver tinsel and mauve floss

Tail Two toppings, a few sprigs of tippet, and kingfisher

Body Two turns of golden silk floss, then golden pig's wool merging into orange

Ribbing Silver twist

Hackle Golden-orange hackle over the wool; red-orange hackle over that, and two or three or more short toppings tied in at the breast instead of shoulder hackle. (These toppings can be as long as to nearly touch the point of the hook. The hackle is applied quite full.)

Wing A tippet feather with a cock-of-the-rock (not the squared feather) on either side, and one above; strips of pintail or wood duck on either side (the barred wood duck is pre-ferred), and as many golden pheasant toppings as you can pile on — seven or eight or more, if you like

Cheeks Kingfisher

Horns Blue macaw

As I copy the pattern for this beautiful fly from the writings of Francis Francis, I admire two dressings of it, one in a glass globe by the noted angler, fly dresser, and historian Brian G. Fabbeni, of Wales, and one by the revered Sydney Glasso, of Washington State, which is shown in Plate V. Fly dressers able to reproduce this pattern correctly are to be congratulated. I think that two tippets should be used in the wing and that they should be as wide as possible to give a high and showy appearance, which is embellished by "as many toppings as you can pile on."

Dr. Pryce–Tannatt calls this same pattern the *Orange Parson*, and Kelson calls it the *Yellow Parson*. Each slightly varies from the original, so for correctness one should follow this Francis Francis dressing. He fished the Erne soon after the fly's origination. The other two gentlemen came later.

Speaking of the Parson Series Francis says,

This is a very showy fly, and is used chiefly on the Erne, but is a capital fly anywhere a showy fly is required. It is on the Erne rather a generic name for a series of flies than for any special one, as we have there Green Parsons, and Blue Parsons, and Golden Parsons, and so on; the Parson being merely significant of plenty of toppings in the wing. The Golden Parson, however, is my idea of the fly.

He also says of the *Golden Parson*, "This is decidedly a *topping* Parson, a sort of bishop or archbishop Parson, in fact, and not for everyday use; we only bring him out when the feelings of the salmon, having resisted all ordinary persuasiveness, require to be very strongly appealed to." Even in those days of abundance it seems, salmon were sometimes so dour that they wouldn't strike at the usual flies. The idea then was evidently the same as today's: tempt them with something different. We call this "experimentation," and it often brings success. I often begin a fishing trip by tying on fresh flies. When new ones don't do well, it's time to experiment with different sizes, different shapes, different colors, and/or different methods. I have learned to keep a few bedraggled, well-chewed patterns for working over dour fish—flies most anglers would contemptuously discard. The results can be surprising!

Many Parson variations featuring toppings and tippets were dressed for or by anglers frequenting the Erne in the years following 1836. Dr. Shiel, Lord Bolingbroke, the Reverend Alfred Meyrick (for whom the Parsons were named), James and Michael Rogan, William Larket, and Mr. Hobson were among these. Here are four more of the original patterns, roughly in their sequence of development. I know of no book which has previously published all of them, even though they constitute an important milestone in salmon-fly development. The first two are variations by Mr. Hobson and Mr. Larket:

Parson No. 2

HOBSON-LARKET PATTERN

Tag Fine silver twist and orange floss
Tail Golden pheasant topping and kingfisher
Body Fiery brown blended into hot-orange pig's wool
Ribbing Medium silver twist
Body hackle Olivy yellow

Wing A pair of tippets, back to back; three red-tipped toppings with tips reaching to tail; two narrow strips of teal, one on each side
Front hackle Claret, wound as a collar
Horns Blue and yellow macaw
Head Black

Parson No. 3

ALSO A HOBSON-LARKET PATTERN

Tag Fine silver twist and mauve floss
Tail Two toppings, tippet strands and kingfisher
Body Three turns of golden

floss; then yellow seal's fur blending into hot-orange seal's fur
Ribbing Silver twist, medium to broad, from golden floss

Body hackle Hot orange from golden floss

Throat hackle Three toppings curved to point of hook

Wing Two tippets back to back; narrow strips of un-barred summer duck (wood duck) on each side; three red-tipped toppings curved to meet point of tail, a cock-of-the-rock feather on each side tied flat; followed by a pinch of hot-orange seal's fur at the base, i.e., like a small head

Side cheeks Long blue kingfisher (These are tied over the little seal's fur head to make the side cheeks stick out.)

Horns Blue and yellow macaw

Both of these patterns are among the earliest ones and are beautifully jewellike in appearance, with very wide tippets and long toppings in the wings. Examples of these are shown on Plate V.

James Rogan (the father of Michael) was actively dressing flies in Ballyshannon at the mouth of the Erne at the time the Parson Series was introduced. He sometimes is given credit for the idea of reversing the toppings in the wings of some of the Parson patterns, although as we have noted, Pat McKay dressed his original *Golden Butterfly* that way, and three of the six flies illustrated in the Reverend Newland's book are done similarly. No one seems sure who first got the idea of reversed toppings, as there are no written records. But James Rogan is given credit for the first of the two following dressings (with reversed toppings), and his son Michael (1833–1905) is credited with the second.

Parson No. 4

JAMES ROGAN'S PATTERN

Tag Gold twist and yellow floss

Tail Two golden pheasant toppings

Body Yellow floss

Ribbing Medium gold twist

Body hackle Pale yellow, wound palmer-style

Wing About fifteen golden pheasant toppings curving upward—use ones tipped with red, if possible—and two blue jay feathers wound on in front

Head Black ostrich herl; black thread

This evidently is the pattern the Reverend Newland calls the *Parson*, as illustrated in the frontispiece of his book.

——————————— *Parson No. 5* ———————————

MICHAEL ROGAN SR.'S, PATTERN

Tag	Flat silver tinsel and purple floss		the beginning of the seal's fur, palmer-style
Tail	A topping, tippet strands, and two small blue chatterer feathers, back to back	*Throat hackle*	Six toppings, tied to curve downwards
Body	Two turns of golden floss silk, remainder of golden yellow seal's fur merging into hot-orange seal's fur	*Wing*	Seven or eight toppings, tied in to curve upward
		Cheeks	A medium-sized golden pheasant tippet feather on each side, about half as long as the wing
Body hackle	A hot-orange hackle wound all the way from	*Head*	Black ostrich herl and black thread

Several other Parson patterns of lesser importance were developed later in an effort to capitalize on the popular trend. Newland says that the Parson Series, with their bright-yellow wings, are intended to imitate shrimps. A modern counterpart might be Colonel Esmond Drury's *General Practitioner*, which successfully uses the same or similar ingredients for the same reason.

The many toppings on most of these flies were very tempting to guides on the rivers. Under the pretext that the flies were overdressed, the guides would "make them more suitable" by breaking off as many toppings as they dared. These would be carefully saved for dressing flies of their own, which they often would sell to anglers. By this means many anglers bought their own toppings back! Some got tired of this petty pilferage and tied their own flies, or had them tied, with yellow poultry hackles instead. No reports exist that they worked any better, or any worse.

Another type of fly, popular on the Erne at the time, is a series called Butterflies. Newland says, "The Butterfly is distinguished readily from all others by its underwings, which, being made of the tippet feather of the golden pheasant tied in whole, give it the appearance of a copper-coloured butterfly." He describes these in dressings featuring red, yellow, green, blue, fiery brown, and claret.

There is inconsistency here. Newland says the Butterflies are distinguished by underwings of *tippets*, while the Parsons are known for "their bright yellow wings formed from six to eight *toppings*." Yet McKay's *Golden Butterfly* has only toppings, while Parsons have underwings of tippets. Only two of these patterns conform to Newland's definition: James Rogan's *Parson No. 4*, sometimes called the *Yellow Parson*, and his son Michael's *Parson No. 5*. Both of these have wings of toppings, as illustrated on Plate V.

The flies mentioned in Newland are all variations of similar ones being tied in Dublin by a tackle-shop proprietor named Thomas Ettingsall, author of *The Green Bank* (1850), which includes an excellent list of Irish flies. Also in Ireland was Cornelius O'Gorman, the supreme fly dresser for the Shannon in those days. The Reverend Henry Newland eventually had most of his flies tied by Michael Rogan (Sr.) who was under twenty years old at the time but who had already achieved local fame for his skills. It is said that Michael was the one who added tippets to the wings of some of his topping-winged Parsons and that he was the originator of the Parsons' name, but as stated previously, there is other evidence that Pat McKay (who evidently was older) anticipated him. Anyway, Newland doesn't mention these developments, so we can assume he was either ignorant of them or that they happened after his book was written.

Newland's tenets may have been correct for the part of the Erne where he fished, when he fished it. But the patterns in question didn't last and evidently were inconsistent with customs elsewhere. His topping-winged Parsons were little used on the Erne but very popular on the Shannon under various other names. The name of Parson remained common on the Erne chiefly to identify what Newland called Butterflies, with wings of tippets topped by toppings. Of these there are many: *Brown Parson, Fiery Brown Parson, Green Parson, Hobson's Parson, Puce Parson*, and *Purple Parson*, plus those previously discussed, and others. These usually have wings primarily of both tippets and toppings. This colorful, distinctive, and sometimes productive winging is popular to this day. The *Durham Ranger* and *Black Ranger* are among numerous examples.

Did these ancient anglers, then, think that salmon struck at butterflies often enough to warrant imitating them artificially? Evidently. But evidence doesn't seem to bear this out, even though the structure of the classic salmon fly seems to support it. My own feeling is that the structure is an elaboration of the trout fly enlarged and embellished to provide anglers with beautiful objects to fish with. Since salmon ordinarily seemed enthusiastic about these forms and colors, the illusion prospered—and isn't that reason enough?

With the Parson and Butterfly series, a third sort of fly was, and still is, popular on the Erne as well as other rivers. This is the mixed-wing type evidently conceived and developed by James Rogan. Newland says of it, "The mixed wing genus has no underwings whatever, but its wings are formed by mixing together the fibres of any description of feather according to the judgement of the maker."

Mixed-wing patterns, of which the various Doctors, *Silver Grey*, and *Green Highlander* are good examples, are composed of a number of single strips of several different kinds of feather. While these can be tied on in a bunch, usually some of the fibres are carefully "married" to one another in a definite order called for in each specific pattern. This provides an opportunity to make wings of bright, medium, or dark feather parts or any degrees in between. Michael Rogan's method was to equalize the ends of the strips from selected feathers and, holding the bunch by its base, to comb them to entirely separate them, to appear much like a hair-wing. Over this he would lay a roofing of feather strips set upright.

While Erne flies were noted for both tippets and toppings, those for the River Shannon usually featured toppings only. Examples are the *Goldfinch* and the *Shannon* illustrated on Plate VII. The *Black Goldfinch* is similar, with a black body. The *Shannon* is dressed in several ways; sometimes with a multijointed body. Yellow macaw often was substituted for toppings. The dominance of yellow and orange on flies for both of these rivers was for greatest visibility, which anglers considered important because of the heavy waters and frequent turbidity.

Flies with the brilliance of Erne and Shannon patterns weren't popular generally, but they did influence the infusion of varying degrees of brilliance into the relatively drab patterns elsewhere. As our story progresses, we will see the growing use of toppings, tinsels, silks, and tippets that transformed salmon flies into jewels of flashing color.

The salmon of each river were often thought to have specific tastes in patterns and colors, so the flies recommended for each river usually had specific common characteristics. For example one river might be noted for fly bodies of fiery brown or brilliant claret, while blue or ash-colored ones were recommended on another. All sorts of diversity existed. The fondness for brilliance was tempered by common sense but was then augmented by the natural desire of anglers to dress their fly hooks with expensive and fetching materials.

One reason for such diversity was that travel then was slow and difficult. Even using railroads, anglers had to get from railheads to rivers with the help of horses. Because rivers were so isolated, fly patterns successful on one usually were unknown or spurned on others. Even parts of the same river had local favorite patterns often unknown elsewhere on the same stream.

Multiply the number of rivers in the British Isles by their parts, allowing that each part or section might generate a range of local patterns, and how many result? The question isn't why there are so many, but why there are so few. Some were called "general flies," meaning they should be accepted by salmon most everywhere, but each part of each river had its special local favorites, and the creation of new patterns and variations, perhaps more beautiful than practical, occupied fly dressers during winter months. If salmon were receptive when such flies were tried, the patterns often became sought-after favorites.

Brilliant Irish patterns weren't confined to the Erne and Shannon watersheds of the western coast. They were indicative as well of what was going on elsewhere on the island. We remember that John Younger noted that such patterns were introduced into Scotland as early as 1810. Yet we jump in this book about three decades to learn what they were. Books about salmon flies, especially Irish ones, were scarce until the 1840s and 1850s. Two more books on fly patterns of special appeal will be discussed in the next chapter. A reason for this paucity has been touched on. In those days in Ireland people who could read and write were rare. The few existing libraries were owned by the clergy, the universities, and by landed gentry and were unavailable to the masses. Information was passed down orally, including lore about fly patterns. Thanks to friends there, a few previously unpublished bits are included in this chapter.

But let no one presume that Irish brilliance in fly design smoldered for lack of written works. Quite the contrary, as we shall see. Take Pat McKay's *Golden Butterfly*, for instance, conceived early in the nineteenth century. At the end of that century (1895) George M. Kelson published *The Salmon Fly*. In it is an entirely different *Golden Butterfly*, whose yellow silk and silver twist body is regaled with *five* black herl butts, *each* veiled above and below with a total of *four* small graduated tippet feathers and crowned with six toppings! This creation is illustrated on Plate XV.

Kelson admits that this *Golden Butterfly* is an "exaggeration" but says it has "actually" killed on the Tweed and Wye, and has hooked salmon trolling on the Tay and in Norway. All I can add is that Victorian fly dressers obviously went to great lengths to imitate a shrimp!

Although this is not intended to be a book about fly tying, it may help to include occasional notes fly dressers might find useful. We have been discussing wings with multiple toppings. How should they be applied to set securely and properly?

When golden pheasant crests are purchased, packing may have pressed their toppings out of shape. Some authorities recommend soaking individual feathers in water (or, better yet, saliva) and drying them pressed around a bottle or other suitable curved surface. Unfortunately, this method can mat the fibers together, impairing the natural veiling of individual fibers which should cascade over each side of the wing. Other authorities prefer holding each feather with pincers over a steam kettle for a few moments. Steaming usually restores natural curvature.

Note that a cross-section of the base of the stem (quill) resembles an inverted triangle. Unless flattened it will slip to one side or the other of the hook's shank. Using a small jeweler's hammer, or something similar, hold the base of the quill against a hard surface and lightly tap it at the tie-in point until the quill is flat. Then nick it at the tie-in point by pressure of the thumbnail against the forefinger to make the feather rise to the desired curve.

Some dressers tie in two or three toppings at a time and thus conserve thread windings. Others do it individually. The important thing is to set each flattened quill base exactly on top of the previous one. Stacking can't be done properly without flattening the quill ends.

Select toppings graduated in length so each one is slightly longer than the one underneath. Each individual crest should be visible rather than all being mixed in a bundle. Topping wings are very beautiful when applied correctly, but it takes practice! If the thread is too thin it may bite into the quills enough to twist them out of shape; if it is too thick, the head will be too big. Experts think stacking a wing of six or eight, or even more, toppings is not difficult. The topping-winged patterns on Plates V and VII are good examples. Notice that topping ends are not trimmed. While salmon couldn't care less, flies with trimmed toppings become outcasts among astute collectors. Select correct lengths in the first place.

CHAPTER FOUR

British Splendor

*P*ATRICK McKAY and Michael Rogan were distinguished innovators both in discerning color combinations and in improving the methods of fly dressing. Pat championed the high, full wing and incorporated abundant color into it—characteristics generally favored in later years. The elder Michael Rogan, the most skillful and ingenious of his fly-dressing family, also excelled in uses of color and innovation. Although his way of blending wing colors and combing them was mentioned previously, more should be said. The selection of these two men for discussion is not intended to denigrate the many others active similarly at the time (Hayes and Rogers of Cork, Ettingsall of Dublin, and O'Gorman on the Shannon, for instance), but their accomplishments appear subjacent.

Michael Rogan (1833–1905) was born and lived near the bridge which passes over the Erne at Ballyshannon, then a famous salmon river and now reduced to angling impotence by hydroelectric structures. He dressed sought-after salmon flies during his early teens and was an accredited expert by the tender age of seventeen. His skillful fingers were surgical in precision, needing no vise, hackle pliers, or any other tools except sharp-pointed scissors and a fine-toothed comb. We have discussed his method of mixing wing fibers by combing symmetrical bunches so the symphony of colors would combine and pulsate in action. How he obtained these brilliant and translucent hues is another story.

Newland complained that the peaty, acidic waters of the Erne faded fly colors to a washed-out appearance, evidently because of inferior dyes. Rogan solved this problem by substituting the ancient dyes of nature, first being sure that the feathers and furs he used were completely grease-free, since the presence of this natural substance encourages fading. This he accomplished (tradition maintains) by storing a barrel of male donkeys' (asses') urine outside his back door and soaking these materials in it. This detergent evidently proved effective, for his flies remained brilliant and permanent in color. What the neighbors downwind thought of Rogan's method isn't recorded, but it seems that he later diplomatically changed to uric acid for degreasing — a similar but less obnoxious solution!

In any event Rogan's two principal accomplishments were his mixed wing and the brilliant, fade-proof colors he developed, colors which even Francis Francis envied but couldn't duplicate. A Rogan characteristic also was that his flies' wings were somewhat longer than usual. His fame as a fly dresser soon reached England. In the early 1870s he was invited for several months at a time for many years to instruct at the (now defunct) London Salmon Fly-Fishers Club and to dress flies for its members.

In addition to the previously given patterns Michael Rogan is famous for two others:

Green Parson

A VARIANT

Head	Black		over the peacock
Tag	Oval silver and red floss	*Throat*	Blue jay
Tail	A topping and strands of tippet, teal, red, yellow, and blue swan	*Wing*	Two tippets back to back, golden pheasant tail, narrow strips of married red-, white-, blue-, and green-dyed swan a bit longer than the tippets, with strips of pintail or teal on each side, and bronze mallard
Butt	Black ostrich herl		
Body	One third orange floss; two thirds green peacock		
Ribbing	Medium oval tinsel and fine oval gold tinsel		
Hackle	Hot orange over the orange floss and yellow	*Crest*	A topping

The *Green Parson* is illustrated on Plate V.

Two notes here seem pertinent: the frontispiece illustration of Newland's book shows a hand-colored artist's rendering of a fly he calls *Jack the Giant Killer*. This also is known as the *Green Parson* and evidently is the original. The entire body is green, and there are toppings instead of tippets in the wing. As noted, Rogan's pattern is a variation of this. Rogan didn't always employ combed mixed wings. This one has whole tippets and strip wings.

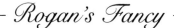

Rogan's Fancy

NO. 2 OF THE BALLYSHANNON SERIES

Head Black

Tag Silver twist and orange floss

Tail A topping and sprigs of tippet and wood duck, with a small Indian crow feather at stump

Body One turn of yellowish-orange wool; the rest dirty reddish claret

Ribbing Silver thread and gold tinsel together

Hackle Same color as body, plus sprigs of tippet tied in rather full at breast

Throat A medium blue hackle

Wing Two of the longest Indian crow feathers, sprigs of tippet, a shred or two of dark wood duck, golden pheasant tail over that, and two strips of woodcock with a topping between

Cheeks Kingfisher or chatterer

Horns Blue macaw

While earlier books may disagree about the proper dressing for this pattern, authorities in Ireland maintain that this is the one Michael Rogan fancied. It is the only one of Rogan's that I have noticed which calls for Indian crow. Fly dressers often varied patterns slightly depending on whim and available ingredients. Another winging for the same fly is as in the *Green Parson*, with the addition of two long jungle cock feathers at center. This seems to be a later variation, because jungle cock was rare in early Irish patterns. Evidently the name *Rogan's Fancy* was a later appellation, because the above dressing actually is No. 2 in the Ballyshannon Series.

Before going on to another Irishman who spread the fame of Irish brilliance to England, it is interesting to note the radical change that gradually occurred in connecting flies to leaders, or "casts," as they are known in the United Kingdom. Up to the 1840s or so, the salmon fly was whipped to a length of looped silkworm gut. When did the eye of single or twisted gut come into use? In 1841 a barrister-at-law named Edward Chitty wrote, under the pen name of Theophilus South, *The Fly Fisher's Text Book*, in which he mentions a knot he recommends "for joining the gut to the loop which is usually made at the head of salmon flies." He also mentions "the loop on a salmon fly head" and "*the fly-head-loop*." There is no assurance, by illustration or otherwise, that this loop was attached to the hook rather than to a length of gut whipped to it. Thomas Tod Stoddart in *The Angler's Companion* (second edition, 1853) says, "one great improvement, of recent date, consists of the substitution, as a mode of attaching it to the line, of a small loop, or eyehole, of gut at the head or shank-end of the hook, instead of a full length of the same material." This "of recent date" is about twelve years after Chitty's book.

This transition seems to have occurred gradually in the 1840s and 1850s, during which time both methods were used. Iron eyes on hooks also became available at about the same time but did not gain popular favor until decades later. One of the surest ways to start a hot argument in any anglers' group was to take either side in the controversy; a very serious one then that seems silly today. Even as late as 1893 an article printed in the British publication *The Field* said, "Whether or not eyed hooks are an improvement on the old gut loops is a point upon which salmon fishers are by no means agreed." We will see that Dr. Pryce–Tannatt in his famous book *How to Dress Salmon Flies* favored the gut loop as late as 1914! Modern dressers of classic patterns add authenticity when they use eyeless hooks with eyes of twisted silkworm gut. Lacking this, violin strings or surgical gut of proper size are acceptable substitutes, but modern plastics are not!

Very near the time in the early 1800s when Pat McKay and the senior James Rogan were originating their brilliant Butterfly, Parson, and mixed-wing patterns on the Erne, an educated Irishman named William Blacker was expertly making his versions of salmon flies in Belfast. Choosing to go where the major action was, he moved to London before 1840 and operated a tackle shop at 54 Dean Street, Soho. In 1842 he published a little book, *Art of Angling*, which professed to give the angler "a perfect knowledge of everything requisite to complete him in this noble art." This collectors' gem is important chiefly because examples of actual flies were wafered between its pages; the forerunner of similar classics, such as W. H. Aldam's "quaint treatise" on *Flees, and the Art a Artyfichall Flee Making* (1875).

Blacker's book, reprinted in 1843, was rewritten and revised in 1855 as *Blacker's Art of Fly Making*. This one lacks the insertions of actual flies but contains twenty copper-plate engravings of flies, fly making, and tackle, of which eighteen are expertly hand colored. Blacker says he stood over the artist to be

W. BLACKER'S

ART OF ANGLING,

and Complete System of

FLY MAKING,

and Drying of Colours.

ILLUSTRATED WITH PLATES,

Shewing the Different Processes

of the fly before it is finished:

GIVING THE ANGLER A

perfect knowledge of every

thing requisite to Complete him in this

NOBLE ART.

PUBLISHED BY THE AUTHOR

W. BLACKER, FLY MAKER,

AND DYER OF COLOURS,

54, Dean St. Soho Sq.re London!

MARCH, 1842.

Title page of Blacker's *Art of Angling* (1842)

sure he did them right. In any event, the results are exemplary. Blacker's volume illustrates and describes fifteen patterns shown on Plate VI.

These fifteen patterns are worthy of special note, of special veneration, in fact. They were painstakingly dressed for me, especially for this book, by Sydney Glasso (1906–1983) of Forks, Washington, an innovative gentleman angler and amateur fly dresser who was a peer of the best who ever have lived. I'm sure Sydney never hooked an Atlantic salmon, but he used similar methods for the steelhead and Pacific salmons near him and he used Atlantic salmon patterns as the basis for dressing flies for those species. When people become opinionated enough to say salmon-fly dressing is a craft that cannot be elevated to art, I only wish they could see Sydney's flies! Sydney was known for many fine touches, especially his tiny fly heads, obtained by concealing windings and only using visible thread at the finish. Having a modesty that excluded any ambition for fame, he could be a model for all of us. As a dedicated conservationist he regretted killing sport fish, saying, "All-out fighters deserve something better than a final blow on the head."

Notice pattern No. 1 on Plate VI, *The Spirit Fly*, of Blacker's. Blacker says of it, "It will be seen to correspond with the shape of the natural dragonfly; and as this fly, of various hues, is reared at the bottom of the water . . . when it leaves the element of its birth, and proceeds to the banks of the river in a very feeble state, directly it receives strength it commences skimming the surface. . . . and, when it comes weakly out of the water, the fish, no doubt, take it freely."

While we may have opinions as to whether or not this *Spirit Fly* resembles a dragonfly, we see here why ancient anglers thought that supposed replicas of the dragonfly should make good artificials, such as were discussed in Chapter Two and reproduced on Plate III. This presumption was widespread then. Blacker says *The Spirit Fly* is so-named "in consequence of its numerously jointed body, its fanciful, florid and delicate appearance. . . . The wings are made of six toppings, with a broad strip of wood duck on either side, a red Hymalaya crest feather at top, a cock-of-the-rock feather, blue kingfisher feather at each side, a black head, and feelers of macaw."

Fly tiers nowadays can reproduce dragonflies much more accurately, but can their work be more beautiful? Another one of this type is Number 3 on the same plate. Still another (not by Blacker) is said to be a descendant of the *Dragon Fly* shown on Plate III. This is the *Erin-Go-Bragh* illustrated on Plate VII. It has been reproduced from Edward Fitzgibbon's *Book of the Salmon* (1850) wherein it is shown in a hand-colored engraving on the frontispiece. Fitzgibbon (pen name, Ephemera) says of it, "This fly is a model of gracefulness, and it will prove exceedingly attractive in pools of medium depth during the late spring, summer, and early autumn months."

Regardless of its intended purpose, I would call this elongated pattern, on its extra-long-shanked hook, a streamer fly, as I would also the Goldfinch and Shannon patterns of Fitzgibbon on Plate VII. So what is so new about streamer flies, which have been presumed to be of much more recent vintage? Streamer flies, regardless of what they are intended to represent, are now considered effective as patterns of last resort; examples of the "something different" which sometimes can provoke action from dour salmon. They can be useful now, but this seems to indicate that they also were useful then!

William Blacker was about forty-five years old when he terminated his fly-dressing and tackle business in Dublin about 1840 and moved to a similar occupation in London. The move was important because he was a principal in converting English and Scottish favor from customary drab fly patterns to the more colorful ones espoused in Ireland. Of course Blacker wasn't the only one to do this, because anglers from the larger island had journeyed to the smaller one long before then, but he was, at least, a prime mover.

Blacker was a leader at an opportune time. This was the heyday of Queen Victoria (1819–1901) when British warships and merchantmen roamed the seas and returned with exotic feathers from foreign lands. It was the heyday too, of sumptuous country houses nestled on vast landed estates where the upper classes enjoyed the best of everything. It was the Victorian notion that possessions should be beautiful as well as functional, a principle that could be easily applied to salmon flies.

Let's take another look at Blacker's fifteen favorite flies on Plate VI. They are less brilliant than Erne and Shannon patterns, but some are more intricate, such as the Spirit dressings Nos. 1 and 3 with their multisectioned bodies butted at their joints by hackles. We see the Erne influence in some of them, such as the Parson variation No. 10. But Blacker favored a trend that was more conservative. Fitzgibbon sums this up in mentioning the Erne and Shannon patterns we have discussed: "The salmon of other rivers despise them. In Tweed water they would be fish frights."

Blacker was a leader and a prophet of future decades. Compare, for example, his favorite patterns with those popular much later, including the classics of modern times. He set a style, or character, which was to become the principal standard as long as classic patterns should remain on salmon rivers.

Blacker must have known Edward Fitzgibbon, who, under the pen name of Ephemera, wrote *The Book of the Salmon* in London in 1850. This, like Blacker's, is a collectors' gem, with five hand-colored engravings of fifteen of his favorite salmon flies and four others of salmon in various stages of development. Like Blacker, Fitzgibbon must have stood over the artist to be sure he got the colors right, because his plates are as accurate as any I have seen prior to the advent of modern color printing. These fifteen patterns are beautifully reproduced on Plate VII by Larry G. Borders, a career airman currently with the United States Air Force overseas.

Several of these patterns are particularly notable. Two are Shannon patterns described here as Fitzgibbon gave them in 1850.

Goldfinch

Body, gold-coloured floss silk; black silk tag, tipped with gold tinsel; ginger-hackle and gold tinsel over body; blue jay at the shoulder, and kingfisher over the butts of the wings, which are to consist of eight or nine golden pheasant toppings of middling size. They should project by half an inch beyond the extreme bend of the hook. Feelers, red macaw; head, black ostrich; tail, golden pheasant topping. [The hook would be about 1/0 regular in modern size.]

Fitzgibbon says that this is a noted fly suitable for low spring, summer, and autumn water in the Shannon, especially on dull mornings and evenings, but that it is too bright for clear shallow water. Note that, in addition to the extra-long wing it has a very long tail of golden pheasant crest extending noticeably beyond the tip of the wing, as is shown on Plate VII.

Shannon

Body, half light orange, half blue silk, to be ribbed with broad silver tinsel and gold twist; a lightish blue hackle, stripped on one side, over body; blue jay under shoulder; head, seal's fur dyed yellow; tag, orange silk; above it another tag of fur of deeper orange hue; tail, large topping; wings, ten or twelve largest size toppings, sprigs of the leading tail feather of the golden pheasant, and four long feelers of blue and yellow macaw. [The hook would be about 2/0, 4X long, in modern size.]

These two patterns, especially the latter, would surely be called streamers in modern parlance. Here, again, the wing projects half an inch beyond the bend of the hook, and the tail is considerably longer, as shown on Plate VII.

During my many years of study of the classic salmon fly, the question often has been asked "What was the first metaled-body fly and by whom and when was it dressed?" The *Silver Wilkinson* has been offered as a candidate for the honor, but that choice appears incorrect.

We remember that Captain Franck before 1658 used "twisted fine threads of gold and silver" in dressing his flies, and we have observed that gold and silver ribbing has been employed ever since, but until Fitzgibbon wrote about it, I never heard of flat tinsel used for fly bodies. He gives the pattern for a "famous summer's evening fly" called *Aglaia*, which is one of a triumvirate of beautiful classics collectively called The Three Graces. It is my candidate for the first metaled-body fly:

Body, all of silver tinsel, ribbed with gold twist; black ostrich tag, tipped with gold; tail, a small topping and a few fibres of the wood-duck's feather; black hackle, thin and short over body, teal hackle at the shoulder. Wings, two toppings, bustard, cream-coloured turkey and wood-duck feathers, and black ostrich head.

Authorities in Ireland have told me that there is oral evidence that Pat McKay was one of the early nineteenth-century fly dressers who knew about this fly, which may date from as early as 1840. I haven't been able to discover the authentic origin of The Three Graces, or who dressed them.

Fitzgibbon offers many old dressings indigenous to various rivers throughout the United Kingdom, including an ancient *Dunkeld*, another version of the famous *Toppy*, and various mixed-, strip-, built-, and whole-feather-winged patterns which indicate that his philosophy of what constitutes an effective mixture of beauty and utility is very similar to Blacker's. I share the wish that he had given his dressing instructions in the modern manner of "first things first," but that isn't the way they did it in those days!

Fitzgibbon must have been a dedicated and peripatetic angler with an inquiring mind, but he evidently lacked ability as a fly dresser. He states that many of the patterns given in his book were contributed by "recognized authorities" such as W. K. Rogers, of Cork, who provided those selected for southern Ireland, and "Mr. Blacker," for northern Ireland. Thirteen of the fifteen he illustrates were dressed by Blacker after he moved to London. "These models," Fitzgibbon said, "will furnish a correct idea of what salmon-flies ought to be in colour, shape and size."

In defense of the large list of patterns he published he says,

> Though there are general flies that will kill in the majority of rivers, they will not always do so, and they must be used only for want of the better [local patterns]. The salmon of every river . . . have favourite flies, some widely differing in size and colour, some less so.

The last is a popular opinion which I think can be carried too far. I believe that an angler can obtain equal results with only a few "general flies" that vary in size, color, intensity (and perhaps in shape). Where and how he fishes them seems far more important than what they look like. I remind myself that I usually carry only about five fly boxes each containing approximately 150 patterns. Then, on the stream, I usually find I lack one or more flies I wish I had! Doesn't everybody?

Having reached the 1850s in our story, we see the Irish preferences in fly design spreading throughout the British Isles but not to the exclusion of the drabber patterns, which also are found at times to be effective. On the Tweed, for example, less colorful flies such as *Toppy*, *Lady of Mertoun*, and *Kinmont Willie* give way to more vivid dressings like *Durham Ranger* (inspired by Parson patterns), *Black Doctor*, and *Dandy*. Since casual observers may not appreciate the intricacy of patterns like these, let's pause to see how they are made and the art and materials required to make them.

CHAPTER FIVE

Classic Materials

$\mathcal{T}$HE "classic" salmon fly purchased from a tackle shop or mail-order house today bears only a casual resemblance to the flies being discussed here. Although it serves its purpose for fishing, it must be made quickly and simply to allow for retail mark-up while still remaining competitive in price. Here, we describe its aristocratic ancestors, now meticulously duplicated to demonstrate how perfection in dressing can approach fine art.

In appreciating the classic flies, we should remember that in the 1800s people had ample time to make complicated classics and sell them directly to wealthy anglers who often regarded their appreciable cost as small change. Then, too, feathers we find expensive or even unobtainable were common and relatively cheap, for they were imported without restriction. Some of the exotic feathers, which will be discussed here, still exist as hand-me-downs from older generations. Fly dressers lacking them can use creditable substitutes, which also will be discussed.

To dress these beautiful counterparts of the classics we come as close to the original ingredients as we can, using old hooks, real silkworm gut, and other Victorian materials and methods whenever possible. Time is not of the essence. Errors are recalled and corrected, rather than being ignored or covered up. If hours are required for satisfactory results in making only a single classic, that is part of the game. The goal is perfection, and the reward an accomplishment that gives expression to one's artistic sense.

Fortunately dressing patterns of the nineteenth century can be learned in easy stages, so don't be awed by the complexity of most of those illustrated herein. Many classics are simple and within the range of beginners. Others fall into the intermediate to difficult class. The patterns shown here illustrate that this hobby can become as involved and challenging as anyone wishes.

Since feathers are the crowning adornment of most classics, let's get acquainted with them first and see what now can be used if, as is probable, some of the historic feathers should prove unavailable. Substitutes always should be employed for practice because many of the original components are now rare and precious. If you want to use traditional dressings for actual fishing, substitutes for rare feathers are more practical anyway. The salmon could not care less!

In the following list of principal feathers the chief country of origin is given, but there usually are others. An asterisk after the name of country indicates that the birds range is widespread.

Amherst Pheasant (*China**)
Readily available.

Blue Chatterer (*Northeastern South America*)
This belongs to the large and diverse Cotinga group, which also includes the cock-of-the-rock and the red-ruffed fruit crow, commonly called the Indian crow. Its small, bright-blue feathers were popular for cheeks and other parts of classic salmon flies, and still are, if obtainable, but feathers are very scarce due to protection, rarity, and cost. Sometimes they show up in inventories of deceased fly dressers.

Seven species of the genus Cotinga are of interest to the classic fly dresser for their lovely, shining, deep-blue feathers. These birds are solitary tropical forest dwellers chiefly native to northeastern South America, Mexico, and Costa Rica. Of these, the Lovely Cotinga (*Cotinga amabilis*), for example, is a bird from about seven to eight inches long which is all blue except for dark-violet patches on throat and chest. These birds' beautiful blue-violet shades are not produced by a cellular structure that reflects light, as in most birds, but by a true pigment within the feathers. In this may lie their popularity for use in exotic salmon flies.

The appellation "blue chatterer" is a misnomer due to ignorance. The bird doesn't chatter; in fact, it hardly ever even peeps. The usually accepted explanation of the name is that the first specimen of this bird to reach Europe was in a shipment of brightly colored skins from French Guiana consigned to Madame de Pompadour (1721–1764), mistress of King Louis XV of France. This courtesan favored unswept bouffant coiffeurs strewn with ribbons, strings of gems, and other decorations, principal among which usually were skins of rare and colorful birds, or perhaps their feathers. The French ship carrying the Cotinga skin(s) was captured by the British and brought to England. George Edwards, the eccentric British naturalist and artist who first painted the bird (from the skin), and other eighteenth-century naturalists, knew nothing of cotingas' habits and behavior and called them "chatterers" because they thought they resembled waxwings. No name could have been more unsuitable.

While the Lovely Cotinga is the best known, and is mentioned by Kelson on page 57 of *The Salmon Fly*, there are at least four others. Lucky is the fly dresser who owns even a few feathers from any of them! Kelson also speaks of the banded chatterer (*C. maculata*), which has darker and more pointed feathers. Evidently he didn't know about *Cotinga cotinga cotinga*, which is darker still and also with pointed feathers, or he would have mentioned it. Also notable are two others: the blue tailed pitta (*Pitta quajana*) and the fairy bluebird (*Irena puella*), both with more rounded feathers.

All these are, or perhaps I should say "were," used in Atlantic salmon fly dressings. Before Kelson and Hale published their books no preference was given between blue chatterer and kingfisher, so the latter may be substituted for the former correctly. One way of distinguishing one feather from the other is that the base of a blue chatterer feather is nearly black, while that of kingfisher is greyish. To my mind, blue chatterer is superior because its tips are more brilliant and sometimes waxy or iridescent. Its rarity recommends use on only the very finest flies.

Substitutions for blue chatterer, in addition to kingfisher, are the head and nape feathers of the blue and yellow macaw or blue feathers from other members of the parrot family. Lacking these, dyed hen feathers might do ordinarily.

Bustard (*Africa*)

This is the common English name for many genera and species of African, European, and Asiatic birds related to cranes and rails whose barred or "speckled" feathers range from tan or cinnamon to dark-brown or black. Before 1838 the bustard was fairly common in England and southeastern Scotland, but later it became extinct there due to hunting pressure. The largest of the group, the great bustard, weighed as much as thirty-two pounds and had an eight-foot wingspread.

Dr. Pryce–Tannatt, in *How to Dress Salmon Flies* (1914) says on page 66, "The richly-freckled wing and tail feathers of various species of bustard (including Florican) and the boldly barred black and cinnamon ones from European species are invaluable for mixed and built wings." Speckled types actually have finely textured barring decreasing in length from spine to edge so fibers appear as speckles or spots. A variety is called florican, or florican bustard, which is descriptive of prominently barred feathers.

Because the birds are so widely distributed, various colorings and barrings in feathers are available and can be selected depending on whatever is called for in specific patterns. Substitutions can be found in domestic turkey tail feathers, peahen saddle feathers, and in some of those found on the now-prevalent wild turkey. A variety in some fly-tying mail-order catalogues is often listed as Speckled Turkey. A florican substitute is silver pheasant tail dyed tan.

Cock-of-the-rock   (*Northern South America*)

This is a plump pigeon-sized South American native so beautiful in its bright-orange or scarlet coloring that it is often compared to birds-of-paradise. Of the two principal species the Guinean cock-of-the-rock (*Rupicola rupicola*) occurs in northern South America, the male being a lovely orange color with touches of brown and white on wings and tail. The Andean cock-of-the-rock (*Rupicola peruviana*) frequents South America's Andes mountains. Its color is more scarlet, with wings tinged with black and white. Both have large upstanding crests of the basic color.

These are members of the Cotinga family, as are also the so-called Indian crow and the so-called blue chatterer. For information on these three families readers are referred to David Snow's *The Cotingas* (Cornell University Press, Ithaca, New York, 1982).

Although angling books rarely distinguish between these two species, the golden-orange Guinean one is usually preferred for classic salmon flies, doubtless because its feathers harmonize with golden pheasant crests. The brilliant feathers were first used in salmon flies in the early 1800s and form parts of the *Golden Butterfly*, *Golden Parson*, and Parsons Nos. 1 and 3, whose patterns are given in Chapter Three. The soft fibers of the feathers are difficult to work with, but their beauty and rarity made them popular for cheeks and wing components. Although the feathers' fine structure cannot be accurately duplicated, dyed webby hen chicken feathers are good substitutes.

We wonder why these Victorians thought it necessary to send to South America for cock-of-the-rock, skins of Cotingas, and other rare plumage. Kelson even specified bird-of-paradise feathers from New Guinea, but he didn't say which colors or which of the many species he had in mind. He may have thought there was only one, and that all its feathers were alike, which is about as far from the truth as one can get! These old anglers wanted exquisite exotics, and the more, the merrier. Nothing was too good for the King of Fishes or, more particularly, for the anglers who coveted him.

Golden Pheasant   (China)

Readily available. Note the dressing suggestions ending Chapter Three.

Goose   (United States, British Isles*)

Readily available. Usually substituted for swan, which is traditional but protected.

Guinea Fowl   (Africa*)

This domestic bird has been widely introduced in the United States and many other countries and is readily available. Its breast and flank feathers form throat hackles on many flies. The body feathers, when dyed *Silver Doctor* blue, often are substituted for blue jay, which is difficult to use.

Heron   (British Isles*)

Since herons are protected in the United States, the long, flowing hackles which give life and character to so many classics, such as Dee strip-wing patterns, are difficult to acquire. Black or grey feathers usually are called for and, if necessary, could be obtained by dying the long-fibered rump feathers of ring-neck pheasants or other birds such as turkeys.

Ibis (Scarlet)   (Northern South America)

While this bird also is protected, its substitutes are so effective that the real thing may be unnecessary. Goose or duck wing feathers dyed pink make excellent replacements, or pink to red undertail feathers of certain parrots, including the scarlet macaw.

Indian Crow   (Northern South America)

The Indian crow, or red-breasted crow, more correctly named the red-ruffed fruit crow, is a black bird somewhat smaller than the common crow and distinguished by a flaming breast of flat-ended, red-tipped, orange-yellow feathers prized by fly dressers for tails, veilings, wings, and cheeks of exotic salmon flies. It is a native of northwestern South America in the areas of Colombia and the Guianas. The word "Indian" is a misnomer arising from early exploratorial misconception. The bird is of the same family, Cotinga, as the blue chatterer discussed above.

This red-ruffed fruit crow is divided into five similar species. The two principal ones are known by the Latin names of *Pyroderus granadensis* and *Pyroderus scutatus*, the difference from our point of view being in the width and color of the tips of the red, scarlet, or crimson ends of the orange-yellow-based ruff feathers. The black feathers from the head and nape are used as body veilings on a very few classics, notably Dr. Pryce–Tannatt's *Black Prince* pattern.

Indian crow is difficult to imitate properly, but a substitution can be made by dying similar breast feathers an orange yellow and using a waterproof pen to add the red tips. Such feathers could be the white ones around the neck of the ring-neck pheasant or small, soft hen neck hackles. Other red feathers also are used; those on the head and nape of the red macaw, for example.

Novice collectors often consider high-grade classic patterns excessively expensive. Consider Pryce–Tannatt's *Popham*, which contains an Indian crow feather in its tail and at least six others in the veilings; not to mention the many other ingredients. If one were able to purchase an Indian crow skin it would contain about 350 usable feathers and (as this book is being written) would be valued at about $700. Thus, each tiny feather would have a value of about $2, giving the *Popham* a minimum value of $14 for the Indian crow feathers alone. Even expert fly dressers often spend at least two hours per complicated fly, redoing various steps to get each one correct. Fifty dollars per fly should seem reasonable for the combination of such materials and craftsmanship.

Jay   (Europe)

The word "jay" in classic fly dressing refers to the European jay (*Garrulus glandarius*), a larger bird than the North American blue jay, which is a protected songbird. Only the striped blue, grey, and black shoulder coverts are used. These are the smaller feathers that cover the bases of the larger ones of the wing. The coverts are barred on one side and must be split so this side only is used for hackle.

The few jay skins available often are inherited and therefore very brittle. One expert recommends soaking them for a few hours in Woolite to make splitting easier. The barred side is short so is suitable only for smaller flies. Substitution is usual, and necessary for larger patterns. Guinea fowl dyed blue is recommended.

Jungle Cock   (Southern India)

More properly named the grey jungle fowl (*Gallus sonneratii*), this is a rooster-like bird of the pheasant family which used to be common in the forests and bamboo groves of the lower mountain slopes and hills of peninsular India.

Everyone interested in fly tying is familiar with the feathers of its cape, with tan enamellike tips and black to white bars. The bird is hunted for its flesh, and the poor natives who need it for food sell the capes for a low price. The demand for their use in fly tying, however, was so great that India put an embargo on export, and both the United States and Great Britain cooperated in 1969 by preventing import. In spite of this, considerable smuggling goes on, but capes, when found, are very high in price.

More recently, jungle cock has been successfully raised in the United States and is readily available, but also at high prices. Until about 1850 it seems to have been unknown in the British Isles, but from then on it is found in a great many classic patterns. Capes possess all sizes of feathers, large ones being used for wing components and smaller ones for cheeks or shoulders. A few of the more exotic patterns, such as *Hale's Evening Star*, use jungle cock for veiling. (Hale gives credit to Kelson for this pattern, but Kelson gives a very different one of the same name.)

There is no satisfactory substitute for jungle cock in classic dressings. Such things as plastic eyes or doctored feathers may do for fishing, but they ruin classics. Lacking the real thing, it is better to go without it.

Excellent capes suitable for classic patterns have most of their feathers unsplit, and the enamellike tips are dark rather than light. Unfortunately, shipments of these capes have usually been picked over by dealers and agents before the amateur dresser can make his selection, so available stock tends to be poor. But here is a way to mend split feathers and improve their color.

Obtain a small bottle of *real* liquid shellac. Pull the required feathers from the skin and stroke the hackles backward to expose the eyes. Put a drop of shellac on the inside of the left index finger tip and puddle it slightly with the inside of the thumb tip. Pick up the feather with the right hand and press its tip into the shellac with the thumb. Draw the tip between the slightly compressed thumb and forefinger several times to work the shellac into the splits. Bad splits may need a little adjusting, but three or four pulls should cement even these and make the splits nearly undetectable. The feathers will dry in a few minutes. Not only will they be mended, they will be stronger, cleaner, brighter, and of better color than before. When dry, the hackles can be stroked back into place.

Do several feathers at once to avoid cleaning fingers often. If soap and water don't clean your skin satisfactorily, use a bit of alcohol. Note that shellac is on the underside of the left thumb and forefinger only, leaving the other hand dry to handle feathers.

Kingfisher   (Asia Minor*)

Of almost a hundred species distributed nearly worldwide, the white-breasted kingfisher (*Halcyons smypnensis*) and the English kingfisher (*Alcedo ispida*) are most commonly used for fly dressing, for which the blue back feathers form cheeks and (more rarely) parts of tails. Kingfisher feathers are widely and correctly used as substitutes for blue chatterer and are often confused with it. Kingfishers are distinguished by long, stout, hornlike bills and grey fiber-based feathers, while similar bases of the blue chatterer are blackish.

Kelson gives an exotic pattern called *The Chatterer* whose body is "Two turns of light violet silk making headway for numberless small Chatterer feathers, closely packed round the rest of the body." Chatterer also is called for in the wings! Kelson must have written this with tongue in cheek, because blue chatterer skins were very expensive, even then. I am sure he really meant kingfisher, as earlier writers usually did.

Books on fly dressing often call for blue chatterer because it is more exotic than kingfisher but in practice even experts use the latter. Some books suggest either. The former is preferred for exhibition patterns due to the prettier waxlike sheen of its feathers. Substitutes for either are the white ruff feathers from the neck of the common ring-neck pheasant dyed medium blue.

Macaw   (South America)

Of the many species, the blue-and-yellow macaw (*Ara ararauna*) and the scarlet macaw (*Ara macao*) are preferred for fly dressing, the former being specified much more than the latter, chiefly for horns, which evidently simulate the antennae of butterflies. Tail feathers are used for these and, since only two fibers are usually needed for a fly, a small piece of tail feather will go a long way. A matched pair of side feathers usually have longer fibers than those on a center quill, so are valuable for use on large patterns.

If one is so fortunate as to obtain a skin of any of these species, many useful feathers will be found, but most classic patterns call for only tail fibers, usually of the blue-and-yellow macaw. Substitutes are white goose or turkey quills dyed blue or reddish-orange.

Mallard   (United States)

This duck's feathers are readily available. The bronze- or brown-speckled shoulder feathers form the roof of many wings and often are applied under a topping. They are also used in strip-wing patterns. The grey flank feathers with their darker grey to black stripes form throats or sides and often are employed in place of scarcer pintail.

Ostrich   (Africa)

Ostrich herl is commonly available and is used on many classic patterns for butts and for concealing the rear dressing of heads. A few patterns call for it as sectional body butts used to cover the anchoring of veilings. The herl usually is dyed black, but sometimes red or other colors. It is considered too soft in the spine for use in wings.

Parrot   (South America)

See macaw.

Peacock   (India*)

Peacock feathers used in classics include speckled or grey-mottled wing quills and eyed and sword-tail plumes. Breast feathers are called for infrequently. Strips or fibers of wing quills are used in some mixed- or built-wing patterns but, since these are hard to obtain, turkey usually is substituted.

Eyed tail feathers, running from bright green to bronze, are occasionally used for butts and heads. Their most spectacular application is in herl wings of a few patterns, the leading example of which is the *Beauly Snow Fly,* wherein large bunches of strands compose the entire wing. Even more beautiful are herl wings entirely composed of strips of sparkling blue-green sword feathers such as are found in the *Alexandra* and *Peacock* patterns. These two types of tail herls are generally available, and there are no substitutes.

Having seen many peacocks raucously strutting on British landed estates, I inquired why speckled wing quills seemed so hard to obtain. I was surprised to learn that peacocks usually live to the ripe old ages of fifty to sixty years. Those that eventually die of natural causes are snapped up by taxidermists who can sell each mounted bird for a thousand pounds or more. That explained the scarcity.

Swan   (British Isles)

Swans of various species are now protected in this country and in the British Isles. Although their feathers are traditional for wings, white goose quills dyed in various colors are acceptable substitutes.

Teal (and *Pintail*)   (United States, Europe)

Since these ducks are hunted, their feathers (dyed, if called for) are readily available. Most used are the flank and body feathers, which are white with black bars. Some are used for entire wings, as on the *Crosfield* and *Silver & Blue*, but usually they make up sides and hackles. In the latter case one side of the stem is stripped off before winding, or a bunch of fibers may be tied on as a "beard." Teal, pintail, and widgeon have very similar feathers, any of which can be used interchangeably, but the teal is more vividly marked. European widgeon is similar to pintail and is preferred on traditional patterns rather than the rather brownish North American species.

Toucan   (South America)

The ariel toucan (*Ramphastos ariel*) is, or was, a common bird in the West Indies and the Guiana region of South America. It is one of numerous similar species noted for its orange, canary-colored, and yellow-red breast feathers and for the dark-red feathers over and under the tail. Historically these were used as tails, tail veilings, body veilings, and throats. More recently these small, bright-yellow feathers are used principally for body veilings, such as in the famous *Jock Scott*, whose body is divided into two equal halves butted between them with black herl and "veiled above and below with six or more toucan feathers."

Captain Hale, in *How to Tie Salmon Flies* (1892) says that "Skins can be bought at the tackle shops." Since this is no longer possible, perhaps the best substitute is the small cup-shaped feathers of the golden pheasant found on top of its crest. Tips of small hen hackles dyed yellow are a common but rather poor substitute.

Turkey   (United States, Europe*)

This common bird's chief value to classic fly dressers lies in the white variety's wing and tail feathers, dyed in various colors if required, which are substituted for swan or goose. The tail, wing, and some body feathers of the brown variety, when proper shadings are selected, are usable substitutes for rare feathers such as bustard. The now-prevalent wild turkey extends this selection.

Widgeon   (Europe)

See Teal, above.

Wood Duck (Summer Duck)   (United States, Canada)

This lovely duck (*Aix sponsa*), once threatened, now is so common that its skins and popular feathers are handled by mail-order houses and material shops. Its black- and white-barred flank feathers and its unbarred breast feathers are used in wings, shoulders or cheeks, and in tails. It also is known in classic literature as "summer duck," "Canadian duck," or "Carolina duck." The mandarin duck's feathers are very similar. When wood duck is specified in fly patterns without added definition the black- and white-barred flank feathers usually are intended. These are commonly applied in strips. Since this duck is rare in Europe, American fly dressers in touch with European counterparts find these an excellent medium for trade.

Feathers are first on this list of fly-dressing materials because the beautiful complexity of classic wings is of principal interest. Beginners should not be dismayed by the difficulty of finding exotic materials. Substitutes always have been used when expedient but, for exhibition patterns, originals increase value and pride of possession. Ignore rare originals, at least until you are sufficiently adept to dress patterns expertly. Start with the best inexpensive substitutes available, and have fun! The attractiveness of the result may be surprising. Many classics are quite simple, and choices can be selected from ingredients at hand.

Hooks

Originally hooks were made by heating a needle or similar larger object until it was soft; then cutting a barb into it and filing the end to a sharp point. The needle then was reheated to form the bend and was tempered so it would bend slightly under stress without breaking. These eyeless hooks (originally lashed to horsehair lines) were attached to lengths of looped silkworm gut and, early in the nineteenth century, to gut eyes, which were used almost exclusively until that century's end. The metal-eyed salmon hook, "a newly invented hook . . . with an eye in the shank," was discussed by O'Gorman in his *Practice of Angling* (1845) but remained unpopular until the end of the century. Dr. Pryce–Tannatt, in his *How to Dress Salmon Flies* (1914) shows seven beautiful color plates of flies, all with gut eyes. Modern classic dressers usually act accordingly. Eyeless (blind-eye or tapered-shank) hooks are readily available. If silkworm gut can't be located, violin "E" strings make acceptable substitutes, each one providing enough for several flies.

All traditional salmon hooks are made with a black japanned finish, usually with the Limerick bend, and (modernly) with an upturned, returned eye when used for fishing or with a gut eye when dressed for display. Light-wire hooks are used for low-water flies. Double hooks, about equally popular as singles for fishing, are rarely used on exhibition patterns because they are difficult to store or display. Some are found on antique patterns.

Dressers of exhibition patterns like to make them appear totally authentic, using all possible ingredients of the past century. For this reason they prefer old hooks which, like exotic feathers, do turn up occasionally. Sometimes they appear on damaged flies stored for a century or more. The flies are stripped down for the hooks, which may need to be made rust free, resharpened, and newly japanned. Connoisseurs can often identify these old hooks by their bends and barbs or other characteristics, and they place greater value on flies dressed on them.

Body Materials

While properly sized and curved toppings might suffice for the tails of simple patterns, they often are augmented by shorter strands or whole feathers of golden pheasant, Indian crow, cock-of-the-rock, jungle cock, blue chatterer, summer duck, teal, swan, and so forth. These often elaborate appendages are placed over the tag, which is of smoothly wound silk held in place by a tip of a few turns of fine silver or gold tinsel or thread. Following these bits of plumed luxury comes the body, wound with dubbing of pig's wool, seal's fur, crewels, Berlin wool, or floss silks of every color imaginable. In later years flat tinsels (usually silver) also became popular.

One example of the devotion the dressers felt for these flies was in the use of pig's wool, a fly-body material that was popular mainly because it was easily available. What was needed was the short and fine hair found on a pig's face. To obtain it one had to shave the pig (supposedly quiet at the time), wash the hair, and pick out the coarse guard bristles. The remaining fluff then had to be dyed many different colors, using organic substances such as the Rogans of Ballyshannon employed. Who would go to all that bother today?

Pig's wool fell into disuse, however, mainly because it was too coarse. Mohair proved too fine and limp, so seal's fur and other substances were employed for fly bodies. Colors needed are bright orange, lemon, fiery brown, scarlet, claret, purple, green, golden olive, dark- and light blue, and black. By blending some of these, almost any shade can be obtained.

Of course even such colorful bodies wouldn't suffice without embellishment. Bodies were decorated partly with tinsels and hackles. Tinsels consist mainly of narrow or broad gold or silver flat, embossed, or oval metallic ribbons, threads, or lace (twist). These often are used in combination as ribbing; five turns spiraled around the body being typical. The best tinsels come from France and are well worth the search and the prices. Those of lesser quality (from India, for example) are readily available. Modern substitutes such as Mylar may suffice for fishing, but they have no place in exhibition patterns.

The fly body is also enhanced (when called for) by palmering a neck hackle around it to give the effect of insect legs and to add action to the fly. This closely follows the ribbing for protection against breakage. Natural badger, furnace, or fiery brown are among the types of hackles used. These sometimes are dyed in many colors, as are white ones.

Bodies often are further embellished by dividing them into two or more parts, each often dressed differently and separated by butts of herl or hackle which may be veiled by such exotics as toucan, jungle cock, chatterer, or Indian crow. Note, for example, the *Baron* pattern illustrated on Plate IX. Its body is in two equal halves of flat silver tinsel and black floss respectively, separated by a black herl butt which is veiled above and below with Indian crow. The previously mentioned *Popham*'s body has three divisions of orange, yellow, and blue floss divided by a rear black herl butt and two similar body butts, all sections being veiled above and below with Indian crow. The *Jock Scott* has a two-section body whose black herl center butt is veiled above and below with six or more toucan feathers. These are typical examples of compound bodies appearing on many classics.

The body is finished with one or two throat hackles of coarse-fibered feathers such as gallina (guinea fowl), teal, mallard, heron, or jay, which may follow a few turns of saddle hackle. Finally, the wing with its satellites of sides, cheeks, horns, and toppings is mounted as outlined in the following chapter. The head is neatly bound with thread, secured by a whip-finish, and varnished to a smooth, shiny appearance. The fly now is complete.

Beginners should not be awed by the multiplicity of feathers and other ingredients required to dress the more difficult classics or by the complexity of many of them. Starting this branch of fly tying is as easy as any other. The difference lies in the greater distance one can go in producing more beautiful and complex results.

If you can tie any sort of fly that can hook any kind of fish, you already have started on the road to perfection. Obtain a classic book on the subject, such as Dr. T. E. Pryce-Tannatt's *How to Dress Salmon Flies*. The scarce 1914 edition has been reprinted in England and is obtainable at moderate cost from angling-book dealers. It contains many simple patterns calling for common ingredients which are easily obtainable. Start simply, and progress as far and as fast as you wish. Take an occasional lesson from a competent instructor. Collect materials gradually and as needed. The fun of dressing classics lies in the pride of mastering increasingly difficult ones while realizing that better results lie ahead.

CHAPTER SIX

Classic Fly Constructions

VICTORIAN angler-author Sir Herbert Maxwell put it rather well when he said, "There is such a mute fascination in daintily dressed salmon flies, their outline so graceful, their tints so delicately blended and so cunningly contrasted, that no nature sensible to beauty can contemplate them with indifference."

Part of the fascination for these classic patterns is in understanding what they are made of and how they are put together, which we will now examine.

During the last century a system was established for describing a pattern by enumerating the successive steps in the application of its parts. Consistency required always using the same names for the same elements. This tradition is still alive and simplifies the art of fly dressing to the extent that anyone who understands it can copy any fly correctly without having seen an actual specimen. The system is the common language not only of fly dressers but of everyone interested in classic patterns. Although experienced readers may consider the following account of flies' components elementary, some will find included in this discussion details not mentioned elsewhere which aid in evaluating quality.

Here are given the definitions of the names of the various parts of a classic pattern in order of their application (simpler patterns don't require them all). The accompanying drawing gives the names of parts of a classic pattern, and Plate IX illustrates the steps in dressing the *Baron*, one of the more famous classics of the late nineteenth century.

Since there are no rigid standards for proportions in dressing classics, readers should refer to older books by experts such as Hale, Kelson, and Pryce–Tannatt to form their own opinions. The answer to correct proportions is to produce results providing an overall harmonious arrangement of symmetrical parts. While expert advice varies slightly, the following should serve as a useful guide:

Tag: A very few turns of fine oval or round tinsel succeeded by a few turns of floss in proportions of one part tinsel to two parts floss, the whole to be no longer than the length of an *average* hook's barb. These are positioned directly above the hook's barb so the dividing line between tinsel and floss is nearly over the tip of the barb. The tinsel sometimes is referred to as a "tip," but listings of

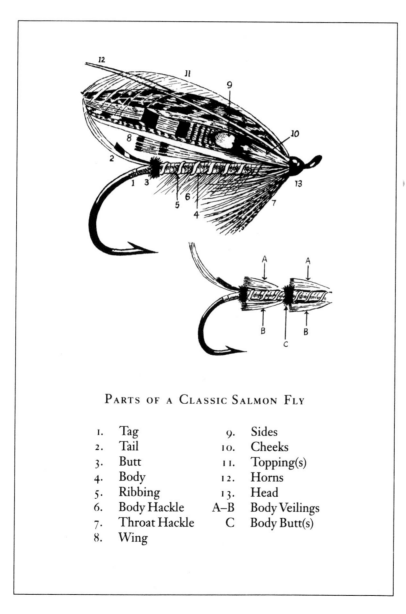

PARTS OF A CLASSIC SALMON FLY

1.	Tag	9.	Sides
2.	Tail	10.	Cheeks
3.	Butt	11.	Topping(s)
4.	Body	12.	Horns
5.	Ribbing	13.	Head
6.	Body Hackle	A–B	Body Veilings
7.	Throat Hackle	C	Body Butt(s)
8.	Wing		

[73]

both ingredients normally are combined as the Tag. The floss acts as an attractor, and the tinsel secures it while also adding a bit of flash.

Tail: On classic patterns this usually is a small golden pheasant crest feather (a "topping") measuring one and a half times the gape of the hook. It curves upward corresponding to the downward curve of the hook's bend. Other feather fibers, or even tiny jungle cock eyes or other feathers, often are added to the tail and sometimes are substituted for the topping. When additional materials are included they usually are half as long as the topping, unless otherwise specified. On relatively simple patterns hair, hackle fibers, or even bits of yarn, etc., are often used.

Butt: This normally consists of two or more turns of ostrich or peacock herl, or of wool or floss, wound on to cover the thread securing the tail. Some authorities think the butt was added to represent the egg sack of an insect, but it is generally considered merely as a decoration. As the drawing shows, it is quite narrow.

Fancy patterns often call for one or more *body butts* separating the body into two or more equal sections, often composed of different materials. A middle body butt can be seen in the illustration of the *Baron* (Plate IX). From this, facing rearward, extend *veilings* of Indian crow; one small feather on top of the body and one below. Other patterns may call for bodies with several butts decorated with veilings of tiny feathers or, perhaps, a turn or two of neck hackle. Meticulous dressers use a tiny hackle brush to stroke the herl's fibers into better outward and backward position.

Body: Patterns may call for a tinsel body; one of floss or herl, or a dubbed one of fur or other materials. Bodies on all exhibition patterns should be smoothly tapered. Dubbing often is described in its successive colors of application. Dubbed ones are picked out with a pin or similar instrument to blend colors and provide a buglike fuzzy appearance. Floss bodies (and tags) should be extremely smooth. I know of dressers who wear white cotton gloves while applying floss, to protect it from roughened fingers and discoloration. Tinsel bodies often are polished after application. Fussiness is important.

Ribbing: This is of flat or oval tinsel, wire, or, in rare cases, colorful thread wound spirally around the body from tail or butt to throat. Sometimes two or more ribbings are called for, usually closely following each other, such as silver lace and silver tinsel. The size or width of these materials should be appropriate to the size of the body. *Five turns* are traditional, because when body hackle (see following) is used it follows closely against the ribbing for protection and more or less than five turns might make the hackling too bushy or too thin. When body hackle is used with ribbing, the ribbing always is oval or round for this reason.

Hackle (body hackle): This is usually a long natural or dyed neck feather palmered around the body as described under Ribbing. It normally is tied in at its point from the second turn of tinsel, headwards to the throat hackle, or to or from a joint. For this, neck hackles usually are superior to saddle hackles because they offer a gradually increasing taper merging in length to that of the throat hackle. Using saddle hackles over the body fails to provide this attractive taper.

Throat (throat hackle): This feather adds to the body hackle (if any) to simulate the legs of a natural fly. It can be a few turns of a natural or dyed saddle hackle wound closely together before or after the wing is applied, or a small bunch of saddle-hackle fibers stripped from the feather and tied in under the hook next to the head of the fly. The latter method often is called a "beard." Saddle hackles usually are employed here because they offer a much thinner quill, which aids in keeping the head small. They also provide the long, soft fibers that look so well, are of uniform length, and provide better action. When the pattern calls for a body hackle, the throat hackle meets and blends with it. It should be as long as or slightly longer than the body hackle, normally extending about halfway toward the point of the hook. Spey patterns and a few others are exceptions, with long, flowing body and/or throat hackles (usually heron) extending to or beyond the hook's bend.

Wing: This is the most characteristic part of a classic fly and the most difficult to apply properly. Wings are of several types, some quite complex, which will be discussed later in this chapter. In the most typical conformation, as exemplified by the *Jock Scott* and the *Green Highlander*, for instance, the wing is equal in height, or width, to the depth of the gape of the hook used. In such patterns it extends to the tip of the tail and borders the curve of the topping, which rather accurately defines its area. Thus, the most typical conformation of this classic type is nearly heart-shaped with the curve of the hook and the base of the throat on one side and the curves of the tail and topping on the other. Notice, however, that the upper side of the "heart" is slightly longer than the other. Visualizing the conventional heart shape is a good guide to proper conformation.

There are exceptions to this conformation. The Rogans started a practice in Ireland of making the wing slightly longer, with sort of a streamer-fly effect. Kelson (see Chapter Eight) preferred a higher, or wider, wing, up to one and a half times the gape of the hook. Specialized patterns often exhibit exceptions.

In reproducing a pattern as given by one authority or another, it is proper to do it in the specified way. In identifying your dressing, it also is helpful to include with the name of the fly the name of the authority you followed in dressing it, particularly if his style is distinctive.

Sides: These embellishments appear on some of the more elaborate patterns and are applied identically against both sides of the wing to occupy part, but usually not all, of the forward portion. Sometimes, if they are slender, the sides extend rearwards, and usually centered, nearly to the length of the wing. They often are of jungle cock or strips of barred wood duck (summer duck); sometimes of married strips of various feathers or, more rarely, of Indian crow, chatterer, or teal.

Cheeks: These very short and small feathers are applied similarly to the sides but, if sides also are called for, the cheeks should superimpose on them while allowing most of the sides to show. Cheeks frequently are the tips of jungle cock feathers, or small chatterer (or kingfisher) feathers, but they also may be small tippets, Indian crow tips, or short feather strips. They may suggest the heads or eyes of actual flies, since they are similarly located. Only on Dee strip-wing patterns are they placed in drooping positions.

Toppings: This is the usual name for the indispensable golden pheasant crest feathers, regardless of where they are used on flies. They are most noticeable when one or more are tied in over the finished wing, hugging and roofing (or "topping") it closely and extending (without trimming) to touch, or nearly touch, the tip of the tail. Properly curved and applied toppings frame the upper edges of the wing, their fibers, or barbs, cascading down both sides of it to produce a glistening golden translucency that provides the beautiful crowning touch on many classic patterns. Toppings also are considered effective attractors for salmon. Suggestions for successfully mounting them are given at the end of Chapter Three.

Horns: In a pair these usually are single fibers of a red or blue macaw tail feather, one tied in on each side of the fly extending over the cheeks or sides to curve backward adjacent to the topping. They are approximately as long as the topping and have a similar curve. If they are a bit longer than the wing they become a focal point. The reason for their inclusion seems dubious, but they are embellishments on fancy flies reminiscent of the "feelers" or antennae of flying insects.

Heads: The final windings of thread to form the head and secure it with a whip-finish need no explanation, but a few points may be pertinent. Critics often start judging a fly by inspecting its head. Is it smooth, with a glossy finish? Is it proportionate to the fly's size? Is it properly tapered and spaced to avoid crowding the eye? Large heads indicate ineptitude, so some experts take pride in very small ones. The late Sydney Glasso, of Washington State, often considered the greatest salmon and steelhead fly tier of modern times, was a master of tiny heads accomplished by concealing thread windings while working overlapping materials forward. Those who have solved the secret are vague about it, as they have a right to be. One must practice and experiment, but results are worth the effort, as Glasso's patterns on Plate VI indicate.

An able exponent of Sydney Glasso's method is Robert Veverka, of Vermont, who called my attention to the presumption that Glasso learned the secret by studying Ernest Crosfield's methods, as illustrated in Eric Taverner's book *Salmon Fishing* (1948). We'll learn more about Crosfield later. He was also judged the greatest salmon-fly dresser of his day, which was around the turn of the last century. For my part I subscribe to the teachings of Crosfield, Glasso, and Veverka. *Granted ample security*, small heads are much more attractive than larger ones.

Having this acquaintance with the parts of a classic salmon fly, let's apply them as an example to the modern way of describing a rather complicated pattern. We select *The Baron* because it contains most of the parts recently mentioned. The assembly of these is illustrated in the eight steps shown on Plate

The Baron

Tag Silver twist and dark red-claret floss

Tail A topping

Butt Black herl

Body In two sections. The first half with flat silver tinsel ribbed with oval silver tinsel and butted (veiled) above and below with Indian crow (extending to tag) and black herl. The second half with black floss, ribs of oval silver tinsel, and having a dark red-claret hackle along it

Throat Jay

Wing Tippet strands, swan dyed yellow, summer duck, blue and red macaw, golden pheasant tail, peacock wing, mallard above and a topping

Sides Jungle cock

Cheeks Blue chatterer (or kingfisher)

Horns Blue macaw

Head Black herl

IX, which was prepared by Ted Godfrey, of Maryland, one of the premier modern artists in the classic tradition. Note that the construction is given in the order of the application of its parts, so that a knowledgeable tier can reproduce it without having seen an example of the actual fly.

Note that this pattern contains thirty-seven separate materials, with the wing components carefully selected, matched, sized, married where necessary, and meticulously applied so that both sides of the fly are identical with matching right and left feather sections. This is only one element of construction. No thread or gaps can show. There are scores of ways to err and only one way to do things right, which echoes a statement of a renowned fly dresser that no one has *ever* dressed a *perfect* classic salmon fly.

This brings up some points I am eager to include. In the British Isles they call people who tie flies "fly dressers." We call them "fly tiers." Both terms should be universal, but there is a difference. To me, a fly tier operates from a utilitarian standpoint. He ties flies to catch fish. A fly dresser operates from an artistic standpoint. His object is to create flies of beauty and perfection. He accepts a challenge that only partly concerns the fly tier. The former is a craftsman, but the latter can become an artist—a "dresser" rather than merely a "tier." Perhaps people who maintain that classic fly dressing is a craft rather than an art are presumptuously unfamiliar with what is being discussed here.

Casual viewers of salmon flies may not realize that they fall into several varieties of construction, but those delving into the subject should want to understand the distinctions because they aid identification and help to define a pattern's history. Salmon flies are grouped by their characters and styles. According to Dr. Pryce–Tannatt, "character" implies a peculiarity of shape and general construction typical throughout a numerous series of flies and thus divides them into common groups or classes. "Character" may be an appropriate word here, but in fact it seems synonymous with "construction." Anyway, it is convenient to divide these groups into two parts: general flies and regional patterns. General flies should be effective everywhere, regardless of where they were originated. Regional patterns are indigenous to specific areas but may of course be effective elsewhere. It may be simplest to divide the general flies into the following seven categories, realizing that some of these can be combined into individual patterns, such as combination of strip-wings, mixed-wings and built-wings, for example.

Whole-feather wings, of which the *Golden Parson*, with wings primarily of a pair of tippets, is an example, are composed of entire feathers set on upright in pairs, back to back; that is, with the outer, or "best," surfaces showing. Such feathers include golden pheasant tippets or sword feathers, jungle cock, etc. Other examples are the *Durham Ranger* and *Candlestick Maker*.

Simple strip wings are composed of sections of feather; usually one section of a right wing feather and a corresponding section of a left wing feather, or the same from opposite sides of a center tail feather. These can be set on in various ways, such as flat, curving downward, or upward and splayed. The popular and simple *March Brown* is an example. Others are the *Blue Charm* and the *Thunder & Lightning*.

Mixed wings are made up of numerous single fibers of various feathers which sometimes are married together (or become so) to form homogeneous sheaths. Embellishments may be added, such as a roof of two matching feather sections. This is the "school definition" but, actually, mixed-wing patterns can be composed of any feathers that are "mixed," as, over the years, the following examples will indicate.

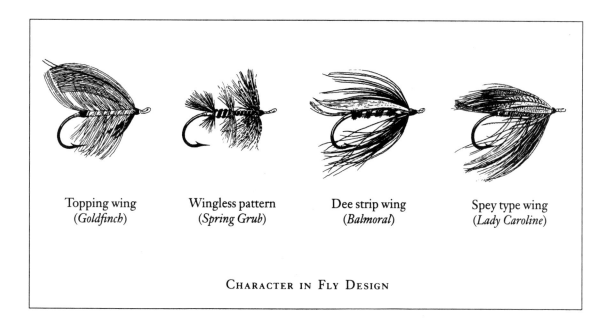

Topping wing
(*Goldfinch*)

Wingless pattern
(*Spring Grub*)

Dee strip wing
(*Balmoral*)

Spey type wing
(*Lady Caroline*)

CHARACTER IN FLY DESIGN

Confusion starts early with William Blacker (c. 1855) and his Erne–Butterfly type which Eric Taverner, a noted authority, calls a mixed wing. Note in Pattern 10 on Blacker's Plate VI that this has a whole tippet feather wing with strip and fiber sides. I would call it a whole-feather-wing pattern, regardless of the mixed sides. In the generation after Blacker, Michael Rogan (c. 1880) dictated that all fibers should be intentionally separated (see page 46). His method produced a *real* mixed wing.

A few years later Captain (later, Major and Colonel) J. H. Hale (c. 1892) advocated laying separate fibers beside and on top of one another to form bunches which were tied in. At about the same time (c. 1890) George Kelson inaugurated the modern mixed wing wherein all the fibers of various sorts were sized and married to form unbroken strips. Finally, Ernest Crosfield, who didn't share Kelson's exotic tastes in feathers and who didn't write much about his methods, evidently dressed his wing by applying very small bunches of fibers, several of which were bound in successively along the forward part of the hook. Those who covet the secret of very small heads, as discussed earlier in this chapter, may gain a tip from this.

Examples of mixed-wing patterns are the various Doctors and the *Green Highlander*. Finally we note that Kelson often combined strip-, built-, and mixed-wing characteristics in the same fly. Such combinations are frequently employed.

Built wings are composed of a foundation of a plain wing of paired upright strips or a whole feather wing. Over either of these are additional strips "built on" by adding one portion after another, like shingles on a roof. In such a wing care is taken that the feather sections underneath are not completely covered by those added later, so parts of all sections will show. Examples are the *Jock Scott* and the *Dusty Miller*.

Topping wings are composed entirely of golden pheasant crest feathers, each usually applied on top of those below by methods such as were explained at the end of Chapter Three. The cascading gold of multiple toppings is reminiscent of spraying fire! Examples of these patterns are the *Goldfinch* and *Shannon* on Plate VII.

Herl wings are made up entirely of fibers or strips from either the eyed tail feathers or the sword feathers of the peacock, tied in one or more bunches. Examples are the *Beauly Snow Fly* and the *Green Peacock*.

Wingless patterns are presumed to imitate grubs and other crawling insects which frequent rivers' banks or beds. They "were found to be of great service particularly when pools have been over-thrashed with winged flies"; a statement from Kelson's *The Salmon Fly* (p. 23) which echoes my admonition to experiment when fishing becomes difficult.

Instead of wings, grub patterns usually have jointed bodies hackled at joint and throat and sometimes at the butt. These hackles usually tilt slightly backward. Grub patterns may have sides, or rudimentary wings, nearly always of jungle cock. Bodies are of wool or dubbing or something similar, with the occasional substitution of tinsel. They are dressed in all hook sizes up to size 1. Examples are the *Wye Grub* and the *Usk Grub* illustrated on Plate XII.

Modern anglers have a tendency to consider the old classics as passé—patterns only to admire, to reproduce as challenges of tying skill, and to treasure as show pieces. These many color plates of outstanding historic examples should not only be considered as things of beauty, but as vehicles providing fly-dressing ideas worthy of modern adoption. The adoption of some, particularly Spey patterns (see Plate XI) and many simplified colorful ones, has led to their very successful use in hooking Pacific salmons and steelhead. Grub patterns are easy to tie, and I don't think they must contain exotic feathers such as jungle cock. The two grubs just mentioned, for example, can be made up in all sorts of sizes and color combinations to provide a wide range of temptations for all sorts of game fish. In Atlantic salmon fishing they suggest ideas for "change-of-pace" patterns that can change a discouraging fishing experience into an exciting and successful one!

Most regions in the British Isles and elsewhere have their favorite wingless, or grub, patterns. Among many, England has its *Wye Grub*, which also is popular in Wales and on other rivers. Scotland has its *Black Shrimp*, Ireland its *Hicks Grub*, and anglers in Wales often favor the *Usk Grub* whose pattern is given below and which is very similar to the Hicks. Since an example may be of interest, this is the dressing for the

Usk Grub

Tag	Fine round silver tinsel
Tail	A bunch of fibers from a red golden pheasant body feather protruding as long as the body
Body	In equal halves: rear half, hot-orange seal's fur with a suggestion of yellow mixed in; front half, black seal's fur
Ribbing	Fine oval silver tinsel
Middle hackle	Between both halves, a small hot-orange hackle followed by a small white hackle, both tilting slightly backward, one turn of each only
Front hackle	Two turns of a coch-y-bonddu hackle with fibers as long as the body
Wing	A pair of jungle cock feathers of same length as the front hackle, tied one on each side to form an upward "V" of about 45 degrees
Head	Red tying thread or red varnish

The *Usk Silver Grub* is very similar except that the entire body is flat silver tinsel ribbed with silver wire.

Hair-wings: To these differences in character, or varieties of construction, I add another, rarely discussed in old angling books but mentioned in Francis' *A Book on Angling* (1880). This is the hair-wing type, long considered to be an American development but used, usually in different forms, in the British Isles and chiefly in the Erris area near the coast of northwest Ireland as early as the middle of the nineteenth century.

The principal form of this type consists of a varicolored floss body separated by as many as five differently colored joints from each of which protrudes in the form of a hair wing a small bunch of differently colored mohair. The length of the bunches graduates from nearly as long as the wing to grow gradually shorter rearward, merging in length with the tail. The wing, throat, and tail usually are conventional. These flies were temporarily popular on Irish waters such as the Owenmore and Lake Conn, and were transplanted from there to Scotland with indifferent success.

Our friends in New Zealand and Australia take pride in their *Matukas* (properly spelled *Matuku*) which are maned somewhat differently by separating the feather or strips-of-fur wing into five or so sections by tying it down with ribbing. Would they be surprised to realize that this idea is about a hundred years older than their "origination" of it?

The other form of this type is a conventional mohair hair-wing dating from about 1840 and evidently originally from the same area. In my collection is an ancient pattern from the collection of the late Otto v. Kienbusch, of New York City. It has a tag of gold tinsel and yellow floss, a tail of toppings, black butt, and yellow mohair body ribbed with oval gold tinsel. The throat and wing are golden mohair, with blue macaw horns. The size is 10/0! A similar but more elaborate pattern is the *Mohair Canary*, evidently transplanted from the Erris area of Ireland to Scotland by Alexander Dunbar, of Inverness not later than 1870.

So what is so innovative about American hair-wing patterns? Were they actually American originations, or did British anglers get the idea many decades before we did?

I noted that these mohair-winged forms were only "temporarily popular" in Ireland and that they met with "indifferent success" in Scotland. A reason was that mohair (Angora goat) is too soft in fiber for effective action. It mats when wet, rather than pulsating as stiffer hairs do. With such innovative ideas, why didn't British anglers hunt around for something more suitable? They could have changed angling history, but we're glad they didn't, because it would have been at the expense of classic patterns.

All general flies have emanated from regional ones such as the various Parson patterns described in Chapter Three. Two types that, while remaining regional, have become more or less general are deserving of special mention, however. Their unusual characteristics are common to two of Scotland's most important salmon rivers, the renowned Aberdeenshire Dee and the famous Spey.

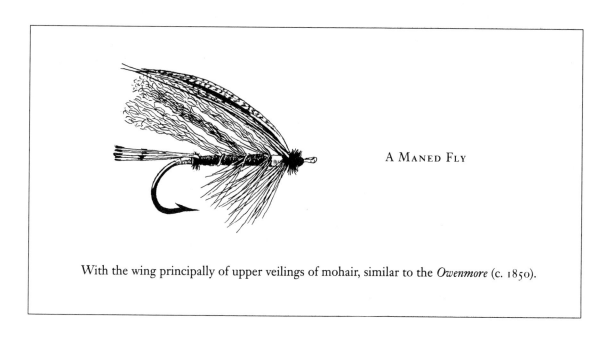

A MANED FLY

With the wing principally of upper veilings of mohair, similar to the *Owenmore* (c. 1850).

Dee strip wings: This distinctive group, examples of which are shown on Plate X, is one of the oldest still surviving. They are tied on specially made long-shanked Limerick hooks to provide a long, yet lightly dressed fly which is unusually large so as to be seen readily and to sink deeper in the deep, rough waters of early spring. Most old Dee patterns have bodies of seal's fur spun on rather loosely; bound tightly by ribbing, and picked out to show a slim core. The picking out of the fur enhances the slimness of the body and provides a luminous effect when the fly is viewed against light. The wings are merely strips (or sections) from the tail feathers of various breeds of domestic turkeys applied splayed in "V"-shape on the upper part of the hook to lie almost flat and slightly separated, low over the body in a nearly horizontal manner. They are tied together at their bases before being set on the hook, so when fished, they break up into separated fibers to allow light to pass between them. Gled (kite) wings were popular until the bird became extinct on Deeside. Hackles are long and flowing, usually of black or grey heron, but sometimes of cock or eagle (marabou), with one side stripped. No Dee strip wing was considered complete without a teal throat; in fact, teal throats were and are considered one of the trademarks of this type.

Perhaps the most famous Dee pattern is the *Akroyd*, distinguished by sides of *drooping* jungle cock as shown on Plate X. It was originated by Charles Akroyd, of Brora, Scotland, in 1878. Brora also is the home of Megan Boyd, Scotland's most renowned fly dresser, who gave me the example illustrated. She says of it, "This fly, given to my father by Charles Akroyd, has black heron [throat] only, but I have seen many old gut-looped *Akroyds* with teal or guinea fowl throats. Charles Akroyd made the *White-Winged Akroyd* too, and I think he made some with guinea fowl and some without. I do know that he nicknamed the fly 'the poor man's *Jock Scott*,' for the body is half yellow and half black." Here is the dressing:

Akroyd

Tag	Silver tinsel	*Hackle*	A lemon hackle over the orange seal's fur; a black heron's hackle over the black floss
Tail	A topping and tippets in strands (fibers)		
Body	First half; light-orange seal's fur; second half, black floss	*Throat*	Teal (one turn, usually)
Ribbing	Oval silver tinsel over the orange seal's fur; flat silver tinsel and twist over the black floss	*Wing*	A pair of cinnamon turkey tail strips (set flat)
		Cheeks	Jungle cock (drooping)

Please note that Mr. Akroyd separated the two body sections by a black butt, which neither Kelson nor Pryce–Tannatt list in components. It's a nice touch, but not necessary. White turkey tail can be substituted in the wing to make the *White-Winged Akroyd*. The fly has been simplified and the orange or yellow and black body has been used in many variations because that combination has proven very effective under varying light and water conditions.

Another popular mid-Victorian type was the Eagles, of which the *Grey Eagle* (Plate X) was popular on the Dee. These were distinguished by long and fluffy hackles of golden (yellow) or grey eagle marabou (now substituted by other kinds), with the usual Dee turkey wing. Variations on this and many other rivers include the *Avon Eagle, Golden Eagle, Hallidale Eagle, Quilled Eagle,* and *Yellow Eagle.*

The Dee was famous for many other patterns varying from the type which has been discussed. In Victorian times the *Gordon* (Plate X) was "lionized." It was originated in the 1890s by Cosmo Gordon, a fly dresser and angler who lived at Maryculter Lodge, near Aberdeen, on the Dee. It was dressed with many slight variations for those who wished it toned down or brightened up. As Kelson says, "No two dressers of today make the fly alike." Another famous one is the *Mar Lodge* (Plate X), originated in the 1890s at a sporting lodge on the Upper Mar section of the Dee. The black center section of the body is sometimes brightened by other colors and these variations are known by other names.

Coincident with or closely following these developments, fashions on the Dee turned to smaller and simpler patterns. The former ones usually were large, often as big as 10/0, and more popular in early season when the water was high and cold and the salmon deep. These latter ones were, and are, more effective for near-surface fishing in warmer weather and are great favorites today all around the Atlantic. Therefore I give three patterns as illustrated on Plate X.

———————————————— *Blue Charm* ————————————————

Tag	Silver thread and golden yellow floss	*Throat*	A deep-blue hackle
Tail	A topping	*Wing*	Mottled-brown turkey tail strips (set upright) and narrow strips of teal along the upper edge; a topping over
Butt	Black herl		
Body	Black floss		
Ribbing	Oval silver tinsel		

Although hair-wing patterns were discussed in my book *Atlantic Salmon Flies & Fishing* and don't belong here, I can't resist saying that the *Blue Charm* in hair-wing style has been one of my favorites all around the Atlantic and especially in Iceland where a fly "with some blue in it" is very popular. Merely eliminate, if you wish, the floss in the tag and make the wing entirely of grey squirrel.

Logie

Tag	Silver tinsel	*Throat*	A pale-blue hackle
Tail	A topping	*Wing*	Yellow swan strips (set upright), slightly covered by brown mallard strips
Body	First two fifths, pale primrose floss, remainder, ruby red floss		
Ribbing	Fine oval silver tinsel		

March Brown

Tag	Silver tinsel	*Ribbing*	Flat silver tinsel
Tail	Unbarred wood duck	*Throat*	Partridge black or brown hackle
Body	Fur from a hare's face (well picked out) or similar dubbing	*Wing*	Hen pheasant tail strips

On the Dee, this fly was a favorite of A. H. E. Wood, the renowned angler of Cairnton, who originated the "greased line" (floating line) method of near-surface wet-fly fishing. He said he could use the *March Brown* all season long and do as well with it as anything else. Well, maybe, but I can think of a few other patterns I might miss. On the average, however, a brownish pattern like this is a sensible selection.

Spey strip wings: Over the hills north of the source of the Dee lies the valley of the Spey, holding a hundred-mile-long river normally of great power. It has given birth to unusual types of flies with individual characters of their own. These flies are of special interest to us, because the mobile action of their long, flowing hackles has proven very effective in attracting not only North American Atlantic salmon but also the salmons and steelhead of our Great Lakes and western coast. American anglers would profit by trying them.

Around the 1850s, as explained by A. E. Knox in his *Autumns on the Spey* (1872) early types were known as various Speals, Reeaches, Kings, and Herons. Let's pass over these for the moment to get acquainted with Spey flies in general.

Spey flies were and are traditionally tied on fine-wire long-shanked Dee-type hooks. They usually have no tag, tail, or butt of any kind. Bodies are wound

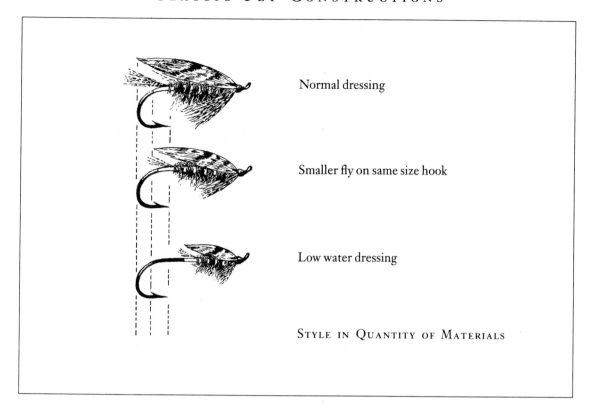

Normal dressing

Smaller fly on same size hook

Low water dressing

STYLE IN QUANTITY OF MATERIALS

thinly, usually with various dullish colors of Berlin wool (a soft woolen yarn) and ribbed with one or two flat tinsels. Spaced between the six or so turns of tinsel is a heron or Spey cock's feather, stripped of the poorest side, and tied in stem first so the longest fibers are at the rear, curving backward. This hackling is protected by turns of silver or gold twist or oval tinsel wound *in the opposite direction* between the hackling to crisscross the flat tinsel. Spey cocks, incidentally, are a particular breed of domestic capon formerly common in eastern Scotland but now difficult to obtain. We substitute other feathers with long, soft, mobile fibers. Throats normally are of teal, widgeon, or guinea fowl. Some tiers wind the ribbing, hackle, and twist in the opposite ways to the above. It seems to make little difference but may depend on which side of the hackle is stripped.

Another distinctive characteristic of Spey flies is the way the wing is applied. The wing is nearly always of short brown mallard strips (sections) and should not extend beyond the bend of the hook. It is applied tied downward to embrace the shank, thus providing sort of a hump-backed effect something like the contour of the bottom of an inverted canoe. Heads are as small as can be made safely. Examples of Spey flies are shown on Plate XI.

Some of the old somber patterns described by Knox are of only scant historical interest, but others survive popularly and effectively, such as the Kings and Herons. We here record only the names of these early flies and give the dressings of two of the survivors: *Gold Speal, Silver Speal, Gold Reeach, Silver Reeach, Gold-green Reeach, Silver-green Reeach, Gold-green Fly, Silver-green Fly, Green King, Purple King, Black King, Gold-purple Fly, Culdrain Fly, Gold Heron, Black Heron, Carron Fly.*

Green King

Body	Green Berlin wool	*Hackle*	A reddish-brown Spey cock's
Ribbing	Flat gold and silver tinsels and		hackle
	gold thread	*Throat*	Widgeon
		Wing	Brown mallard strips

Grey Heron

Body	First third, lemon Berlin wool;		each slightly separated
	remainder, black Berlin wool	*Hackle*	Grey heron
Ribbing	Flat silver tinsel, very sparse,	*Throat*	Speckled guinea fowl
	and oval silver and gold tinsels,	*Wing*	Brown mallard strips

Spey flies were tied with various minor variations. There was no such thing as a constant dressing, and even the same people often dressed specific patterns somewhat differently from time to time. The old dressings were popular into the 1870s, but more gaudy ones gradually appeared such as the various Doctors, *Jock Scott, Butcher,* and *Delfur Fancy,* as well as hair-wings such as *Arndilly Fancy* and the *Munro's Killer.*

When I last fished the Spey, on the Seafield water in the late 1970s, a few rods selected classic patterns, but most of us flaunted tradition in favor of hair-wings or even tube flies. It was June and the river was down, so small sizes (2s and 4s) proved successful. My most powerful rod was a nine-foot Cortland graphite, which had been at least adequate in Canada and elsewhere for salmon exceeding twenty pounds, but it was treated with polite scorn by the ghillies and with condescending tolerance by our hosts.

During riverside conversations I maintained that the rod was suitable for usual conditions and was more fun to use than the fourteen-footers customarily wielded on the Spey. This opinion proved partly right but mainly wrong. Even in June, the winds sometimes blew snow and rain showers sideways to collapse casts frequently. On those days the longer double-handed rods rolled out "Spey casts" (sort of elaborated roll casts) with reasonable efficiency, while I had the choice of learning their methods with borrowed rods or sitting streamside to observe the action. The answer is obvious. Be armed for both methods. Scotland's weather, even in early summer, isn't always for bluebirds!

A classic salmon fly's character, as we have said, has to do with its peculiarities of shape and general construction. Although the descriptions I have attempted are necessarily rather involved, they should provide better familiarity with this important subject. There is a distinction between character and *style*, and the latter can be treated much more briefly.

Style concerns only one pattern at a time and the several different ways it can be dressed for varying fishing conditions. Since we have cited the *March Brown* previously, let's use it again as an example.

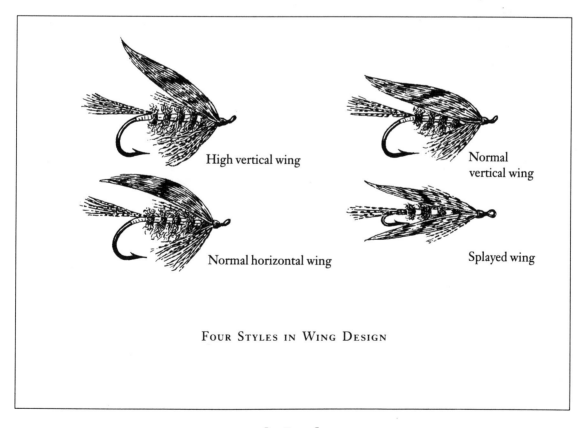

High vertical wing

Normal vertical wing

Normal horizontal wing

Splayed wing

FOUR STYLES IN WING DESIGN

Imagine dressings of it on two identical hooks, but one in sparse style in which a minimum of materials is used, and one in overdressed style where more than the usual number of ingredients are crowded on. The sparse style will sink faster and perhaps deeper than ordinary for deep-lying fish. The overdressed style might be preferable to the ordinary dressing if you want the fly to work very near the surface or perhaps to skitter in the manner of a riffled or hitched fly. I remember occasions when I worked flies over salmon without result until, in desperation, I skated the fly with a long surface wake and got immediate results.

Of course, another style is the low-water one in which a very small dressing is applied only to the forward half of a hook that could hold a dressing several times larger. Such styles are handy for low-water fishing when tactics similar to the "greased line" are used.

Then, if the pattern allows it, strip wings can be applied to hug the body; dressed abnormally high, or curved upward rather than downward. They can be dressed splayed, or horizontally, as well as vertically. Thus, our *March Brown* can be tied in a wide variety of styles, according to whatever the angler considers appropriate for existing conditions.

I don't think the weight of hooks has much effect on sinking the fly. It is the amount of dressing that matters.

CHAPTER SEVEN

The Welsh Influence

REGARDLESS of local fishing quality, anglers appreciate the lure of different rivers, particularly when they hold abundant salmon. So it was that Francis Francis (1822–1886), author of *A Book on Angling* (1867 and five later editions) and called by R. B. Marston "the most distinguished angling editor *The Field* ever had," often journeyed from his home in Devonshire to the small city of Usk, in Wales, to fish the river of the same name. Then, the river Usk was "one of the best managed in England, and perhaps more salmon fall to the rod there than nearly all the other English rivers put together."

In addition to that enticement there were others. The Three Salmons Hotel at Usk, dating from the seventeenth century, with its coach house and stables, stands only a few hundred yards from the river. As a "fishing hotel" it was a favorite and frequent meeting place for anglers of note, including several to be discussed later: George M. Kelson, Dr. T. E. Pryce–Tannatt, Sir Herbert Maxwell, and, of course, our present subject, Francis Francis.

I like to envision some of them reclining comfortably before a glowing evening fire in the oak-paneled gathering room, chuckling over their ale or whiskey at the defensive explanations of the one who most recently fell in, or the enthusiastic description of the new fly pattern that hooked "the big one" that day. I like to envision this camaraderie with the serving maids scurrying about, one perhaps answering with a concave reflex and a blushing remonstrance the friendly pat or jab of one of the anglers as she deposits a filled tankard on the ancient oak table beside him.

A special point of interest at the Three Salmons was the corner of the room. For a great many years and until very recently it always contained a fly-dressing table and cabinet of materials for anyone's use. Since each angler was expected to replace at least as much as he used, the enviable hoard annually got bigger and bigger.

Prominently clamped to the table was a handsome vise made in the early 1800s by the Messrs. Holtzappel, of London, with small vertical steel clamps adjustable for height to a brass clamp base. This vise was in frequent use by the guests named above, as well as by many others of different distinctions. It is known that Kelson used it to originate or reproduce many patterns, including his famous grubs, such as the *Usk Grub*, also called the *Spring Grub*. When this fly-dressing corner was eliminated a few years ago, the manager of the Three Salmons Hotel sold the famous vise to my old friend, Brian G. Fabbeni (then of Usk) who gave it to me. As this is being written, the Three Salmons vise is being exhibited with part of my collection at The American Museum of Fly Fishing, in Manchester, Vermont. While modern vises are more efficient, surely there exists none with more historic associations!

A frequent member of these gatherings was A. D. Berrington, chairman of the Board of Conservators for the Usk and many other Welsh rivers during a large part of the last half of the past century. He advised guests of the Three Salmons as to water conditions and productive pools, and it was chiefly due to him that the Usk became one of the best managed and most productive salmon rivers in Wales. His granddaughter, Baroness Gwen van Moyland, loaned essentials of Mr. Berrington's salmon-fly collection to Brian Fabbeni so that he could expertly reproduce prominent examples for this book. Some of these patterns are shown on Plate XII.

Brian Fabbeni is an artist, historian, and eminent amateur salmon-fly dresser who refuses to use substitute materials. So, for example, since the *Bittern* pattern centered in the top row of Plate XII required two feathers from the now endangered bittern, he visited a museum and cajoled the curator into opening a case so he might pluck two selected feathers from the stuffed bird!

The *Bittern* also should be noticed because while it is typical of the moderate simplicity of early Welsh patterns dating before 1850, it is still in popular use today. Stylistically it is similar to Hansard's *Spring Fly* and *Summer Fly* on Plate III, which Hansard evidently borrowed from Bainbridge's *Fly Fisher's Guide* (1816). George A. Hansard, author of *Trout & Salmon Fishing in Wales* (1834) says that these two flies depict most people's belief of what Welsh salmon flies looked like in those days and that "The flies ordinarily used by the native Welsh angler are very sober in color and few in number." He goes on to suggest that the reason

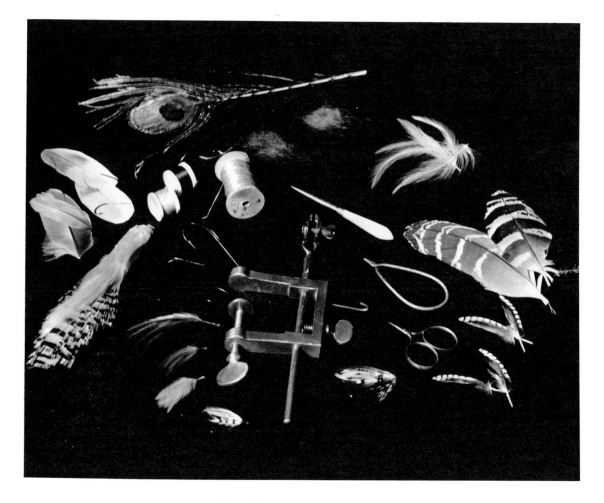

THE THREE SALMONS VISE
AND FLY DRESSING MATERIALS AND TOOLS
OF THE VICTORIAN PERIOD (C. 1880)

Surrounding the vise (from lower left, clockwise) neck hackles, hooks, golden pheasant,
macaw, parrot, silks, tinsel, peacock tail, pigs wool, saddle hackles, stiletto, hackle pliers,
scissors, florican bustard, blue jay and two completed flies.

for this was that Welsh anglers had no access to exotic plumage in the distant
and wild parts of Wales. Most of the old Welsh patterns then were tied with thick
bodies made of strands of tweed and wool from the Welsh mills and plumage
from wild birds of the Welsh marshes.

Francis says about Welsh flies around midcentury, "The hackle is always long
and is wound up the body in a very close spiral. The wings are set on Tweed-wise
and consist of strips applied separately so that they project beyond the hook, like

slightly opened blades of a pair of scissors." Simple palmered patterns also were popular. "The palmer-flies of Wales are dressed on two hooks, the second and shorter one being whipped, back to back, on top and half-way down the shank of the longer one."

Over the years, however, with colorful ingredients available, some Welsh patterns become brighter and more complicated, as examples on Plate XII indicate. During the latter part of the nineteenth century visiting anglers such as Francis, Kelson, and Pryce–Tannatt obviously accelerated this tendency. Kelson surely introduced his exotic high-winged patterns, so I have included his *Captain* in the center of Plate XII. Elaborate flies such as this evidently were mostly thought unnecessary because simpler ones did well enough. Francis, however, describes two other quite different flies also named *Captain*. One of these has a body with four joints, each butted with a cock-of-the-rock feather wound on as a hackle and each of different body colors ribbed with gold thread. He says this was used on the Welsh River Dovey and, since he also describes other complicated patterns, there must have been at least a moderate trend toward them late in the century. Francis also describes a simpler dressing of a different *Captain* which will be given in his manner later in this chapter. It is somewhat similar to the *Gamekeeper* illustrated on Plate XII but contains peacock sword fibers, which I think make it more attractive.

Francis was a man anglers could envy. Since he enjoyed independent means he could and did devote all the time he wished to fishing. In this engrossing pursuit he was unusually versatile, delving into various types of angling, from river, lake, and pond bottoms to surfaces with various forms of tackle which employed all sorts of baits, lures, and flies. These efforts culminated, as they do with many of us, in the specialty of fly-fishing, first for trout and ultimately for salmon. They culminated also in a great interest in salmon flies, some of them very exotic, as those from his book, and illustrated on Plate XIII, demonstrate.

Francis Francis was born in Devonshire in 1822 as Francis Morgan, the son of a Royal Navy captain. His step-grandfather, whose family name was Francis, left to him a sizable inheritance with the stipulation that he must adopt the grandfather's name to receive it; hence, Francis Francis. After a moderate education and a stint at engineering he devoted himself to the sporting life, mainly to angling and to writing fishing literature. He was a frequent contributor to the prominent British sporting publication *The Field* and later became its respected angling editor. He wrote several books, notably *A Book on Angling*, upon which we soon will comment. He died in 1886, at the age of sixty-two.

Perhaps because of these varied interests, Francis Francis may have lacked the expertise in salmon-fly dressing exhibited by such other angling giants as Kelson and Pryce–Tannatt. But he could dress a very presentable fly and was the originator of several relatively simple patterns. Of these, two, illustrated on Plate XII, are contemporary favorites:

Francis' Favourite

Tag Round medium silver wire

Tail Golden pheasant crest, with a small bunch of golden pheasant tippet fibers (This is the tail as tied on the Usk fly. Other patterns show, instead of this, a few sprigs of red ibis.)

Butt Black ostrich herl

(eliminated on some patterns)

Body A few turns of yellow wool or seal's fur, the rest of dark claret

Ribbing Fine oval gold tinsel or gold thread

Throat hackle Coch-y-bonddu, tied to reach point of hook

Wing Sections of dark speckled turkey

Berrington's Favourite

Tag Flat gold tinsel

Tail A few strands of scarlet mohair, golden pheasant tippets, and a small jungle cock's feather tied flat on top (the latter often eliminated)

Body Fiery-brown seal's fur

Ribbing Flat fine gold tinsel, closely ribbed

Hackle At throat, coch-y-bonddu, tied full

Wing Sections of rich brown turkey wing, with one slip of white-tipped turkey in between, tied short and upright; the tip of the wing not to go beyond the length of the body

Francis says, "I killed a good many fish a few years since on the Usk, and all with one fly, which was then called Francis' Favourite." The story goes that he tied this fly on the banks of the Usk between 1865 and 1870. It reminds me, if dressed in the popular American hair-wing style, of the *Black Bear*, with a colorful butt, yellow, in this case.

This fly, used by Mr. Berrington and Francis Francis on the Usk, was said to have "accounted for a lot of salmon from that river." History has it that Francis dressed these two typically Welsh patterns on the same day, the latter during the evening, using the famous vise in the gathering room of the Three Salmons Hotel.

Francis says, "The Usk flies are not gaudy as a rule, plain yellow-orange, and olive wool bodies with turkey or peacock herl wings and lightly tinselled rule the roost." Large sizes "for high water are of a tawny yellow . . . rather rough, some heavily tinselled, some lightly, and some without any. The tails are mostly a twitch of scarlet mohair, with a bit of tippet or jungle cock; the hackles of a dirty-brown red hard upon cinnamon, one or two with a turn of black at the shoulder; the wings are either plain brown speckled turkey, bustard, or bunches of peacock herl."

Smaller sizes for low water have bodies that "are of warm orange wool; tails as before; pretty closely tinselled; with coch-y-bonddu hackles, only black at the butt . . . ; wings either of dark rich brown turkey, or a bunch of herl."

Such descriptions were true into the latter part of the nineteenth century, but only partially true after that, when visiting anglers introduced gaudier patterns and more exotic materials became more available.

Although the Usk is the focal point of this account, the patterns being described were among the usual selections on the many other salmon rivers of Wales. We shouldn't forget that grub patterns (several developed by Kelson at the Three Salmons) were popular for summer fishing on all the rivers and that, perhaps as a change of pace, they should be popular as well on rivers everywhere today. The oldest Usk pattern (the forerunner of several) is the *Usk Grub*:

Usk Grub

ORIGINAL PATTERN

Tag Flat gold tinsel

Tail Tips of two Indian crow feathers (or a few red over orange feather fibers)

Body Alternate bands of lemon yellow and black chenille

Hackle Tied in at the halfway point of body and wound palmer-style to the front. Coch-y-bonddu hackle followed by three turns of larger coch-y-bonddu hackle in front. The front hackle is as long as the body and graduates smaller in line with the base of the tail

Head Black thread, varnished

The usual hook size for this pattern is 1, or 1/0. It reminds me of a North American fly sometimes called the *Teagle Bee*. It often is successful everywhere, not only for Atlantic salmon but also for other salmons, steelhead, and other species of trout. It can be fished both dry or wet. A later dressing of the *Usk Grub* is found in Chapter Six.

Three other historic Welsh favorites merit special mention. This one, named for the late Lord Llanover, whose estate near Abergavenny on the Usk still produces some of the finest salmon fishing in Wales, is typical of popular patterns there during the last half of the preceding century:

The Llanover

Tag Silver twist

Tail A topping and ibis

Body Two turns of bright-yellow pig's wool or seal's fur, merging into deep orange and then into medium red claret and finally into darkish blue. The claret and blue are picked out for a roughish effect

Ribbing Flat gold or silver tinsel, sometimes followed by gold twist

Hackle A dirty coch-y-bonddu hackle at shoulder, sloping back to point of hook

Wing Mixed; brown mottled turkey, bustard, pintail, blue, yellow and claret swan (the blue most plentiful); a topping over all, and blue macaw horns

Head Peacock herl

Another pattern especially popular on the rivers Tave and Cothi, is:

The Trewern Tickler

Tag	Flat gold tinsel (two turns)	*Wing*	A tippet feather or a small bunch of tippet fibers, roofed with brown mallard
Body	Dark- to medium-blue wool (or floss, in smaller sizes)		
Hackle	Black, palmered over forward two thirds of body	*Throat*	Blue jay
Ribbing	Flat gold tinsel (optional)	*Head*	Two turns of black ostrich and black thread

Note that this pattern has no tail. The wing, with its tippet fibers roofed with mallard, is similar to old Irish mixed-wing patterns such as were dressed by Michael Rogan, as discussed in Chapter Three. In smaller sizes, this is a noted sewin (sea-run brown trout) pattern. Wales is still noted for its sea-run brown trout, many exceeding ten pounds in weight. The best fishing for these is at night, which can make for a rather sporty proposition. Previous daytime familiarity with river conditions is strongly advised!

Perhaps the most famous of all Welsh patterns is the *Evans Fly* described as early as 1841 by Edward Chitty (pen name, Theophilus South) in his *Illustrated Fly Fisher's Text Book*. I see no reason why it should be more successful than others given here, but correspondents in Wales and Ireland say it still is "one of the finest low-water flies (in all sizes) to this day," which is a rather good record after about 150 years. Perhaps we should give it a swim!

Evans Fly

Tag	Fine silver wire and yellow floss		above these twelve fibers of striped (or mottled) turkey, roofed with brown mallard
Tail	A topping		
Body	Mulberry floss	*Throat*	A blue jay hackle tied collarwise in front of the wing, sloping backward
Ribbing	Fine silver wire		
Hackle	Tied close under wings, a small dark partridge		
Wing	Twelve fibers of tippet, three or four fibers of green parrot,	*Head*	A collar of black ostrich herl, finished with black thread

Modern practice in Wales is to eliminate the turkey from the wing. Note that the throat is applied to the right of the wing (after the wing is mounted), which is common in Welsh fly dressing.

Thus, Welsh salmon flies progressed from the drab and often unidentified "barnyard types" of earliest fly-fishing to the brighter and more exotic ones of the middle and late nineteenth century, but the progression didn't stop there. As the next three chapters will show, most rivers in other parts of the British Isles already boasted colorful patterns featuring complicated construction and fancy ingredients. Anglers on these Irish, English, and Scottish rivers introduced examples of such general patterns to Wales, where they vied with simpler ones in popularity. Inspection of fly books on any reaches of the dozen or so most prominent Welsh rivers would find in them classics such as *Black Doctor, Black Dog, Britannia, Butcher, Gordon, Jock Scott, Sir Herbert,* and *Wilkinson,* among many others.

Doubtless the simpler patterns did fully as well, but it is the inveterate tendency of anglers everywhere to favor exotic complexity. This favoritism is abetted by the inclination of authors to publish exotic patterns, which was precisely the practice of the group frequenting the Three Salmons Hotel, of which the earliest writer was Francis Francis.

Francis wrote his *A Book on Angling* in 1867 and through five editions, expanded it from 429 to the 520 pages of his sixth and final edition, published in 1883 three years before his death. These were followed by at least one other edition, edited by Sir Herbert Maxwell in 1920. Of the fourteen chapters in the sixth edition, one is on salmon fishing and three on salmon flies. The others include four on bottom fishing and coarse fish, plus information on trout flies, spinning for trout, lake fishing, tackle making, and so forth.

Since many readers are specialists who may want parts, but not all of Francis' volumes I wish that, with so much time and knowledge at hand, he had broken his work down into two or more parts, one devoted exclusively to salmon flies and fishing. His four chapters on this subject are well worth the cost of the big book, however, which despite adulterations, is still considered an essential work.

Not only this. In his various editions Francis adds patterns of some salmon flies while dropping out others that may have had historic value to us. He also sometimes varies dressings. For example, the *Jock Scott* calls for blue chatterer cheeks in some editions and either kingfisher or jungle cock cheeks in others. Both blue chatterer or kingfisher *and* jungle cock should be used, as the pattern near the end of this chapter makes clear.

In his sixth edition Francis gives over a hundred patterns, some not found anywhere else. In defense of this (as if he needed any!) he says, "There are many persons who hold that half a dozen flies are enough to kill salmon on any river in the kingdom, and will despise the notion of such an extended list of flies. To such irreverent scoffers and heretical unbelievers I have nothing to say. Let them indulge in their repertoire of a bit of old Turkey carpet and a live barn-door rooster."

Since Francis' last edition was published a year before George M. Kelson began his series of articles in the *Fishing Gazette*, in which he originated the modern system of progressively explaining the dressing of fly patterns, that important innovation doesn't appear in Francis' book. This is unfortunate because modern fly dressers must translate Francis' vague instructions into modern parlance, often losing essential details in the process.

Let's take as an example the previously promised dressing of one of the versions of the *Captain*, quoting Francis' method of explaining it. This pattern is regional to the rivers Teifi and Towey in Wales. Francis' explanation:

No. 4, THE CAPTAIN—Tag, gold tinsel; tail, a topping and a few sprigs of sword feather; body, dark orange crewel; fine gold tinsel; common red hackle all up, with some brown mallard, and long sprigs of sword feather tied in at breast; wing, two tippet feathers with darkish bittern over.

This is an attractive and easy pattern to dress and is reminiscent of the Parson patterns described in Chapter Three. But Francis' old-fashioned instructions lack the precision and orderly clarity which modern dressers expect and which are necessary for faithful reproduction.

Some of the patterns Francis provides seem extravagantly ornate, as examples on Plate XIII show, but such embellishments were esteemed during the latter half of the nineteenth century. Then, intricate and brilliant originations burgeoned into so many hundreds (or even thousands) that this book can show only a scant sampling. Note, for example, the *Indian Crow, Shannon,* and *Nicholson* patterns on Plate XIII with their multicolored body sections separated by several vivid butts and veilings! These were considered deadly salmon tempters, on the assumption that the salmon possessed the same exotic taste as the anglers themselves.

Two more sensible patterns on this plate are particularly noteworthy because they seem to be ancestors of modern popular ones. They are given as Francis recorded them, but in a more lucid current manner.

Highlander

Tag	Silver twist and gold floss	*Body hackle*	A pea-green hackle from floss to throat
Tail	A topping	*Throat hackle*	Blue jay
Butt	Black ostrich	*Wing*	Sprigs of tippet, with mallard and pintail over, and a topping
Body	Two or three turns of gold floss followed by yellow pig's wool and dirty green mohair, the latter picked out	*Cheeks*	Double jungle cock on each side, the outer ones shorter
Ribbing	Flat silver tinsel	*Head*	Black

This pattern was popular midcentury and later in the Ness region of Scotland on rivers flowing into the Moray Firth. It is important because it evidently was the forerunner of the popular *Green Highlander.*

Doctor

Tag	Fine gold twist (three or four turns)	*Throat hackle*	Brown grouse or partridge
Tail	A topping	*Wing*	Mixed, bustard, dark turkey, Argus pheasant and claret, blue and yellow swan (the latter predominating). ("In smaller flies mallard and pintail can be included.")
Butt	Scarlet crewel		
Body	Pale-blue floss		
Ribbing	Narrow flat silver tinsel followed by silver twist		
Body hackle	A medium-blue hackle wound from tail to head ("This is varied at times with blue jay's feather.")	*Head*	Scarlet crewel

This, most surely, is the original *Blue Doctor,* given its color designation to differentiate it from its later variations, particularly the *Black Doctor* and the *Silver Doctor.*

While most of the patterns discussed in the next three chapters are of this period, the middle and late 1800s, we shouldn't pass on without honoring what is perhaps the greatest fly of them all, certainly the most popular classic of all time, the lovely *Jock Scott*. While it is discussed in many other books, none seems to have given it the true and detailed account it so richly deserves. First, the correct pattern, as given by Jock Scott to Forrest, of Kelso on Tweed:

Jock Scott

Tag Silver twist and yellow silk

Tail A topping and Indian crow

Butt Black herl

Body In two equal sections: No. 1, of yellow silk (buttercup color) ribbed with narrow silver tinsel, and butted (veiled) with toucan above and below, and black herl; No. 2, black silk ribbed with broad silver tinsel

Hackle A natural black hackle, from center

Throat Gallina

Wing Two strips of black turkey with white tips, golden pheasant tail, bustard, grey mallard, peacock (sword feather), swan dyed blue and yellow, red macaw, mallard, and a topping

Sides Jungle cock

Cheeks Blue chatterer

Horns Blue macaw

Head Black herl

George Kelson (see Chapter Eight) calls the *Jock Scott* "the utmost triumph in harmony and proportion" and stresses that yellow silk should be used instead of substituting orange which, when wet, turns a dirty brown. Discoloration also is avoided by using white or yellow tying thread under the yellow part of the body.

One of Jock Scott's employers, under the pen name of Punt Gun, published Jock's obituary in issue number 2095, dated February 18, 1893, of *The Field* ("The Country Gentleman's Newspaper"):

> To all salmon anglers the name of Jock Scott is such a household word that I feel no apology is needed to your readers, many of whom have killed dozens of fish with this fly, for inserting a notice of the inventor, whose name it bears, on his death, which took place on January 24th, 1893 at Langshaw Cottage, a shooting lodge belonging to the Earl of Haddington, overlooking the valley of the Tweed, which he loved so well, and in whose silvery stream the first specimen of his fly was tried.

John Scott, better known as Jock, was born at Branxholme, Roxburghshire, in February, 1817, and began his sporting career at the early age of thirteen, going into the service of the then Marquis of Lothian under the head keeper, Robert Kerss, at whose able hands he first learned how to tie a fly. Here, however, he only remained two years, at the end of which time that prince of Border sportsmen, the late Lord John Scott, happened to see him and, taking a fancy to the look of him, asked his name and, on his saying Jock Scott, offered to take him into his service. This offer Jock readily accepted, and remained there for twenty-seven years, namely, to within a short time of the lamented death of his lordship. After a year or two spent tying flies for sale, he became keeper of Lord John's intimate friend and brother sportsman, the present Earl of Haddington, in whose service he died.

Jock was of the true hard Border breed and, though not a big man, had a frame and constitution of iron, which (had not an incurable malady seized hold of him during the last two years of his life) looked like landing him into his nineties, and well he wanted it for, as a constant attendant for years on one of the keenest and hardiest sportsmen the Borders ever saw, he was at it night and day with otter hounds, rod or gun, deer stalking in the Highlands and fishing in Norway, and spent nearly as much of his time in the water as out of it.

It was while acting as fisherman to Lord John at Mackerston in 1850 that he set himself to devise something new and taking; the *Jock Scott* was the result and, on trying it himself, he was so pleased with it that he gave a pattern to the late Mr. Forrest, fishing tackle maker, Kelso, who one day, I think at Bemmir-ride, after trying a lot of flies in vain, put it on and with such marked success that he thereupon named it after the inventor and, as "Jock Scott," it will remain while salmon swim in Tweed. With Jock's death has passed away another link with the old days when a sportsman was, at any rate, to be a man. May he rest in peace.

It is said that the *Jock Scott* is the first salmon fly to employ jungle cock in the wing, a statement challenged by the *Durham Ranger* (see page 112).

Some accounts have had it that Jock originated the fly while he and his employer were on a steamer to Norway, which evidently isn't correct. In my collection is a 2/0 *Jock Scott* as nearly perfect as any classic can be. It was dressed (from memory) by the great Scottish professional, Megan Boyd, of Brora while I watched and photographed her. It took exactly thirty minutes, which is probably a record for this grade of work.

Many patterns have imitated the half yellow and half black body of the *Jock Scott*; notably, among the classics, the famous *Akroyd* Dee strip wing. This divergence in body coloration seems to attract salmon under nearly all conditions, which may be why the modern hair-winged *Rusty Rat* is so effective.

To end the present chapter, a short note on the fly tackle Francis Francis used between 1850 and 1880 may be of interest. This consisted of a ferruled (not spliced) greenheart rod between eighteen and twenty feet long equipped with an eight-plait, tapered-silk line which was well dressed. This was "state of the art" in those days because "plaited" (braided) lines were usually of silk combined with horsehair, the silk predominating, and often were level instead of tapered, except for fine fishing. The tapered line didn't lay out as well in opposing winds, but heavy (level) lines were more inclined to soak up water until anglers learned that they could be oil-dressed. The end of the casting part of the line was tapered from treble to double gut, and then to stout single gut "close upon four yards" in all. Reels were dismissed briefly by Francis because, in those days, they merely served to store line. They were called "winches." "The winch should be the common or check winch . . . capable of holding 120 or 130 yards of line."

The Welsh influence on classic salmon-fly design has been minimized while we have concentrated our focus on the progress in other areas of the British Isles, so the attention paid in this chapter has been well deserved. While rural Welsh patterns may have been necessarily simple, we have seen that visiting anglers introduced reasonable color and complexity, as the examples on Plate XII indicate. These presage the advent of the Golden Age soon to come.

CHAPTER EIGHT

The Golden Age

FRANCIS FRANCIS concisely sums up fashions in flies during the latter part of the nineteenth century: "From 1840 onward a rivalry was set up on many English and Scottish rivers between the old drab patterns and the new gaudy invaders from Ireland, the usual result of which was the defeat of the native flies or at least their partial suppression. On some rivers the revolution did not take place until much later—as late as 1890."

It seems that fashions had more to do with this than the fastidiousness of fish, which I'm sure were attracted to rustic patterns as easily as to the more exotic varieties. Evidently George Mortimer Kelson would have agreed with this, but he didn't say so because that would have been contrary to his book which, for nearly a hundred years, has been the arbiter of gaudy patterns.

George Kelson (1836–1920) was a controversial Englishman more maligned than applauded. His reputation was his own fault, as we shall see. He wrote the keystone tome *The Salmon Fly* (1895) and a smaller also-ran called *Tips* (1902) as well as many angling articles in the British periodical *The Fishing Gazette*, starting in 1884. George was a highly experienced angler and an unusual character well worth meeting.

Kelson has been called the Grand Old Man of Salmon Fishing and the High Priest of the Salmon Fly. He probably would have agreed wholeheartedly with these and similar accolades, because his many good qualities lacked modesty. He was the self-styled supreme authority on all matters concerning salmon fishing, particularly flies. He fished in as many far-flung rivers as he could reach and chalked up a record of landing over three thousand salmon. Thus, he was possessed of vast experience and was highly skilled as a tackle expert, caster, and fly dresser. He was a hardy man, fond of practical jokes, wagers, and good living. If his line became snagged when a fish was on, he thought nothing of stripping and swimming or wading in icy water to retrieve line and fish.

Let's picture him as he portrays himself in an illustration in his book. Of average height and build, he is dressed in stocking-foot waders, a short tweed jacket, and a bowler hat waterproofed with size and Acme black, with his casts (leaders) coiled around it. He is neatly bearded and wears a very long moustache, carefully waxed at its points. His favorite Farlow greenheart rod rigged with its light narrow-spool Patent Lever Winch rests against his shoulder while he knots a fly to his cast.

Kelson had his faults as well as his virtues, and the former got him into serious trouble with R. B. Marston, the experienced and ethical editor of *The Fishing Gazette*. Kelson and Marston began as friends and fishing companions, but they didn't end that way, largely due to Marston's resentment over Kelson's claim to have developed fly patterns traceable to others. Marston could have quietly refused to publish such material. Instead, he decided to fight it out in print, fully aware that controversy was the fertilizer that sustained his periodical's growth.

As previously stated, Kelson began writing for *The Fishing Gazette* in 1884, and the trouble evidently began a year or two later when Marston reviewed Kelson's book. Kelson considered that Marston had damned it with faint praise, the reason evidently being that Marston believed Kelson had claimed many originations to which he had no right. And so, it seems, there was a brooding atmosphere as the years went by.

These embers burst into flame in 1908 when Kelson was seventy-two years old. The matter centered around the origination of numerous patterns Kelson had attributed to himself, his father, or his friends. In rebuttal, and in print, Marston said, "His [Kelson's] book is supposed to give the history of certain salmon flies. I say that some of these he claimed to have invented or named were neither invented nor named by him [Marston documents examples]. . . . Kelson claimed he was the inventor of making salmon flies with mixed wings. Salmon flies with mixed wings were made before he was ever heard or thought of. . . ."

Of course Kelson didn't invent the mixed wing, as we learned in Chapter Six, and perhaps he didn't mean to maintain that he had, but he did originate a variation of it.

There's much more to these altercations but, since they seem trivial, let's let them rest. Kelson had so much going for him, not only in flies, but in tackle and angling-apparel development, in fishing methods, and in his books, that one

GEORGE MORTIMER KELSON

as illustrated in his book *The Salmon Fly* (1895)

[107]

wonders why he should have been accused and found guilty of petty falsifications. Marston may have damaged or even destroyed Kelson's reputation during his lifetime, but Marston now is forgotten except for yellowed pages in libraries. On the other hand, Kelson's book *The Salmon Fly* (1895) continues to grow in fame as a cherished collector's classic and fly-dresser's guide. It contains 240 lucid salmon-fly patterns, with 8 color plates illustrating 52 historic flies. The plates are stylized artist's conceptions, lithographed originally on stone, and lacking pictorial accuracy. The original edition, now very scarce and costly, was faithfully reprinted in 1979 by The Anglers & Shooters Press, of Goshen, Connecticut.

The question arises, did Kelson consider these exotic flies necessary to the exclusion of simpler ones? A point rarely published, and which Kelson should have stressed in his book, is that he used very few patterns and that he regarded the many in his book as serving an historical rather than a practical end.

It is clear, however, that Kelson loved magnificent and intricate patterns, as so many of us do now, and for the same reasons. To dress them is a challenge, and we collect them because they are rare and beautiful. We do so regardless of what we prefer for fishing. In his articles for *The Fishing Gazette* (but not in his book) Kelson gave the patterns for several flies which he credited to Major John Traherne, one of the great salmon anglers near the end of the last century. Lest they pass into obscurity, I give three here, and illustrate them on Plate XV.

Juno

Tag	Silver twist and blue silk (the same color as the cheeks)	*Ribbing*	Silver lace, and silver tinsel
Tail	A topping	*Throat*	Blue macaw
Butt	Black herl	*Wing*	Golden pheasant toppings, seven or more
Body	Orange silk halfway, the shade like the rind of a darkish orange, and yellow silk the same tone as the hackle	*Sides*	Jungle cock
		Cheeks	Kingfisher
		Horns	Blue macaw
Hackle	Yellow macaw, from the yellow silk	*Head*	Black herl

By "silver lace" Traherne and Kelson refer to "silver rope" or "cord," or, as we now term it, "oval tinsel." Kelson calls the *Juno* a "magnificent" pattern whose "harmony is simply superb." These words of praise also could be showered on the next two by Major Traherne:

Gitana

Tag	Silver twist, and red silk of the same color as the points of the Indian crow
Tail	Two toppings; jungle cock and kingfisher, one of each on either side
Butt	Black herl
Body	One-third silver tinsel; over which four Indian crow, two at top, two at botton, back to back, sideways (as veilings); continuing with three or four close turns of black herl. The rest black silk
Hackle	Black, from silk
Ribbing	Silver tinsel, and gold lace
Throat	Green macaw (the feather is from under the wing or tail of the bird)
Wing	Two dark-blue macaw feathers (taken from the top of the wing), jungle cock on either side extending beyond tag, and five tippet feathers, reaching to the butt, with three or four golden pheasant toppings over
Cheeks	Enameled thrush
Head	Black herl

If macaw can be obtained by a capable dresser, he has a prize in this pattern. Evidently "enameled thrush" is similar to blue chatterer or kingfisher except that it is chocolate color. The five tippet feathers (on each side) are graduated in length, the outer black bar of each smaller one covering the second black bar of the larger one (see Plate XV). Kelson says this "is a good spring pattern for the Tay, Tweed, and Shannon; also first-rate in Norway!" (The exclamation point to this remark has been added!)

These three patterns are illustrated at the top of Plate XV and are included for readers who wish to attempt beautiful and complex historic classics. They never before, to my knowledge, have been found in books. Kelson says in *The Fishing Gazette* that this fly was the subject of much "chat" during the evening of a day when a quintet of anglers each killed a heavy salmon with one. We avoid comment!

Quinchat

Tag Silver twist, and purple silk (same shade as throat of blue chatterer)

Tail A topping

Butt Black herl

Body In five sections, each increasing in length. The first part is red silk, the same shade as the points of the Indian crow, with one of these feathers (as veilings) above and below. The remaining four divisions are light-blue silk, the same color as the light-blue chatterer hackles, and the second and third veiled above and below with blue chatterer hackles from the top of the tail. At the end of the fourth and fifth divisions the veilings are light-blue macaw

Ribbing Fine oval tinsel

Throat Yellow macaw (flank feather)

Wing Two blue macaw feathers

Sides Two green macaw feathers (two thirds as long as the wing feathers)

Cheeks Indian crow. Two toppings over

Horns Red macaw (double)

Head Black herl

Kelson gives in his book a pattern for a *Golden Butterfly* which is entirely unlike the historic Pat McKay original illustrated on Plate V and which evidently has nothing to do with it. To avoid confusion and also because Kelson's is very beautiful, his is illustrated on Plate XV. He says he got it from Major Traherne, who originated the three preceding patterns. These four outstanding classics make me wish that the major had written a book of his own.

Golden Butterfly

Tag Silver twist and light-blue silk

Tail A topping

Butt Black herl

Body Light-yellow silk. The body is divided into five sections, butted at each with two tippet feathers (back to back) above and below, slightly increasing in size (from rear), as well as black herl

Ribbing Three turns in each section of fine silver twist

Wing Six toppings

Horns Blue macaw

Head Black herl

This fly should be dressed on a long Dee hook to accommodate the five body sections and their veilings. Kelson calls it an "exaggeration," by which he evidently means that it is better as an exhibition pattern than for fishing, but he does affirm that it has killed salmon on Tweed, Wye, and Tay. Perhaps!

Kelson fished the Tweed frequently but doesn't describe the most interesting historic fly developments there. The few he does mention are somewhat in error. Without belaboring this, let's examine an example or two.

First, to recall the Tweed flies' history a bit. In Chapter Two, the old-fashioned Tweed flies such as *Lady of Mertoun* and the famous *Toppy*, espoused by Younger and Scrope, were described, and are illustrated on plate IV. For others early in the nineteenth century we might turn to the forty-two patterns given by Henry Wade in his *Halcyon* (1861), eighteen of which are shown on Plate VIII. Hot on the heels of this book, and preceding it in some places on the Tweed, came the revolution in fly patterns from drab to gaudy mentioned in the first paragraph of this chapter. The transition, of course, was gradual. That it was well marked is indicated even by some of Wade's more colorful examples. These generally are rough originations lacking in the precisely harmonious styles under midcentury development. Wade seems a bit behind the times because, when his book was published, this transition was strongly in progress, at least on the lower reaches of the hundred-mile-long River Tweed.

Developments on this part of the Tweed centered around the towns of Kelso and Sprouston. Sprouston was the home of James ("Jemmy") Wright (1829–1902), considered the most innovative and artistic fly dresser for miles around. Jemmy Wright wasn't content merely to duplicate and sell patterns as they existed. He obtained samples of competitors' work and studiously undressed them to learn secrets and expose errors (even as experts do today). His little cottage and tackle shop was a daily gathering place for anglers interested in the latest news about flies and fishing.

Nearby Jemmy's place was the Sprouston (Angling) Club formed in 1845 by several fly-fishers including Mr. Walter Scruton of Durham and Mr. William Henderson (1813–1891), author of *My Life as an Angler* (1876). Since Mr. Henderson and Mr. Scruton were fishing buddies, the former's statement that the latter originated the famous *Durham Ranger* at the club will have to stand, in spite of Kelson's claim that James Wright originated it. The fact that Mr. Scruton resided in the town of Durham helps confirm this. Mr. Scruton evidently got the idea from one of the Parson patterns, such as the *Golden Parson*, described in Chapter Three. He added jungle cock to the wing, a feather not well known previously. We learned in Chapter Seven that the *Jock Scott*, often said to be the earliest pattern containing jungle cock, was originated in 1850. Mr. Henderson says he caught a big salmon on the *Durham Ranger* in 1846, however, so it was originated before then.

Neither of these gentlemen provided the original pattern, but it varied very little in versions published later by Francis, Kelson, and Pryce–Tannatt, so it won't be repeated here. Note on Plate XVIII that the second black bars of the base tippet feathers are placed directly over the butt, and that the outer black bars of the covering tippet feathers are superimposed on the second black bars of the base tippets. The jungle cock feathers, showing most of tips only, nearly touch the meeting point of the tail and the topping. Dressers often fail in this. The fly is beautifully illustrated in Pryce–Tannatt, and his dressing seems most attractive.

Although James Wright didn't conceive the *Durham Ranger*, he did originate the *Black Ranger*. These were followed by several variations, including Blue, Red, Silver, and Gold. In various accounts of Wright's prowess as a fly dresser he is given credit for several other prominent patterns. Not all can be documented to him, but evidently he was responsible for the *Thunder & Lightning* ("the great storm fly"), the *Black Doctor* (a variation of the older blue one), the *Greenwell*, and the *Silver Grey*.

James Wright also was partially responsible for the early version of the *Silver Wilkinson*, if we can give his pattern that compliment. Mr. Henderson says about this, "[in 1843] I directed Jemmy Wright to dress a fly with white silk body, golden-crest wings, blue chatterer shoulders and grey tippet. . . . Some years afterward the idea of a white-bodied fly was improved upon both by Mr. Greenwell and Mr. P. S. Wilkinson, each inventing a fly whose distinguishing characteristic was a body formed of silver tinsel." There seems to be only vague similarity between Wright's version and Wilkinson's, if any. The *Silver Wilkinson* is almost like the *Silver Doctor*, except for the magenta throat and a few embellishments. Pryce–Tannatt says that no two people dress the fly alike. There is controversy as to whether this was the first one with a silver body. Some opt for *Aglaia*, one of the Three Graces noted by Fitzgibbon (Ephemera), which was described in Chapter Four.

Kelson's book is a general one covering tackle and fishing methods as well as fly dressing and fly patterns. Although it is a prime classic for any angling collection, other works such as Hale's and Pryce–Tannatt's excel it in instructions on classic fly dressing. Kelson's chief value lies in his clear and orderly instructions

Color Plates

PLATE II

The Twelve Flies from
The Treatyse of Fysshynge wyth an Angle

Attributed to Dame Juliana Berners (1496) Dressed by Jack Heddon, England

No. 1
The Dun Fly
(March)

No. 2
Another Dun Fly
(March)

No. 3
The Stone Fly
(April)

No. 4
The Ruddy Fly
(May)

No. 5
The Yellow Fly
(May)

No. 6
The Black Leaper
(May)

No. 7
The Dun Cut
(June)

No. 8
The Maure Fly
(June)

No. 9
The Tandy Fly
(June)

No. 10
The Waspe Fly
(July)

No. 11
The Shell Fly
(July)

No. 12
The Drake Fly
(August)

While these flies were intended for trout, they occasionally hooked salmon. The *Treatyse* says, "The Samon is the most stately fyssh that ony man maye angle to in fresshe water. . . . Ye may take hym: but it is seldom seen with a dubbe (an artificial fly) at suche tyme as whan he lepith." Salmon were formidable for the tackle of the time, but these patterns influenced salmon-fly design for at least 250 years.

PLATE III
Primitive Patterns to the Early Nineteenth Century

The Horse-Leech Fly
(Simpson)
First mentioned by Barker (1657) and by Chetham
(1681). "They are of various colours."

The Dragon Fly
Also named *Libella*
or *Libellula*. c. 1750
(Simpson)

Another
King's Fisher Fly
(Simpson)

The King's Fisher
or
Peacock Fly
c. 1750
(Simpson)

An Unnamed Pattern
First dressed in 1775
(Simpson)

A Double-Winged Fly
described in
The North Country Angler
c. 1786
(Alcott)

The following five patterns were illustrated
in Bainbridge's *The Fly Fisher's Guide* (1816)

Spring Fly
(Alcott)

Quaker Fly
(Alcott)

Gaudy Fly
(Alcott)

Summer Fly
(Alcott)

Wasp Fly
(Alcott)

As tackle improved, salmon flies began to take on character of their own, graduating from trout patterns and those originated for pike. Early examples supposedly imitated dragon flies. George A. Hansard, in his *Trout & Salmon Fishing in Wales* (1836) says these lower five patterns long remained standard on North Welsh rivers; were sober in color and few in number, with large hooks and coarse dressings. For later Welsh patterns see Plate XII.

PLATE IV

Dressed by Alex Simpson, Scotland

First Fly   *Second Fly*   *Third Fly*

Fourth Fly   *Fifth Fly*   *Sixth* (or
                                           Maule) Fly

The Tweed Patterns of John Younger
as described in his
River Angling for Salmon and Trout (1840)

Michael   *Toppy*   *Meg in*
Scott   *Her Braws*

Meg with the   *Kinmont*   *Lady of*
Muckle Mouth   *Willie*   *Mertoun*

The Tweed Patterns of William Scrope
and published in his
Days and Nights of Salmon Fishing (1843)

Early-nineteenth-century British salmon flies (except Irish ones) were simple and drab, made from ingredients gleaned from barnyard or glen. These twelve early Tweed patterns were typical of those popular on other rivers, with exceptions such as Spey flies and Dee patterns; also generally drab but often distinguished by long, flowing hackles, as illustrated on Plates X and XI.

PLATE V

Irish Patterns of the Victorian Era

Dressed by Brian G. Fabbeni, Wales,
except for *Golden Parson* by Sydney Glasso

Black Goldfinch
Hayes of Cork
Pattern

Golden Butterfly
Pat McKay's
Pattern

Rogan's H. I. S.
Ballyshannon
Set No. 5

Parson No. 1
Pat McKay's
Original Pattern

Parson No. 2
Hobson-Larkett
Pattern

Parson No. 3
Hobson-Larkett
Pattern

Parson No. 4
James Rogan's
Pattern
(Yellow Parson)

Golden Parson
Francis Francis'
Pattern

Parson No. 5
Michael Rogan Sr.'s
Pattern

Green Parson
A Later Variation
c.1850

Ballyshannon No. 1
Michael Rogan Sr.'s
Pattern

Ballyshannon Puce
William Blacker's
Pattern

Claret Jay
Hayes of Cork
Pattern

Shannon Goldfinch
Rev. Henry Newland's
Pattern

Fenian
Hayes of Cork
Pattern

Meanwhile, around the 1800s, Irish salmon flies became ablaze with "gaudy" colors, featuring the shining yellows, black-striped oranges, and reddish hues of the golden pheasant, plus other rare and brilliant plumages, mainly from South America. Irish dressers such as Blacker and Rogan introduced these to anglers on the larger island, where at first they were spurned as "fish-frights." The beauty of these exotic patterns, however, proved irresistible.

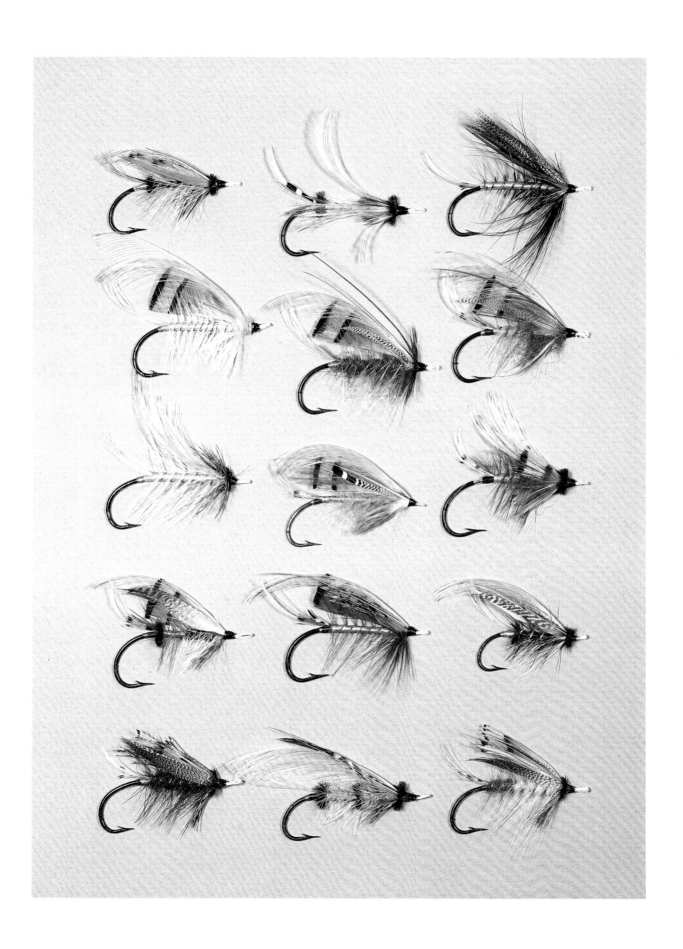

PLATE VI

Patterns from
William Blacker's *Art of Fly Making* (1855)
Dressed by Sydney Glasso, Washington

No. 1
The Spirit Fly

"Its colours will be found most enticing to the fish, and is a sister fly to *Ondine*, in the *Book of the Salmon* by 'Ephemera'."

No. 2
No Name

"This is about as fine a specimen of a Salmon fly as was ever thrown into the water, and will kill Salmon and Grilse in every Salmon river in Great Britain."

No. 3
Another of the Spirit Flies

"... that kill as well in the rivers of Ireland and Scotland, at high water, particularly the Spey and Tweed."

No. 4
A Celebrated Claret Fly

"... of very killing qualities both in Scotland and Ireland, and in the Thames as a trout fly."

No. 5
A Brown Fly

"... a general favourite among the 'old ones,' on every Salmon river in Ireland and Scotland. No. 6 may be used in a similar manner."

No. 6
A Silver Grey Fly

"... a great favourite on the lakes of Killarney for Salmon and Grilse, and for Sea and white Trout."

No. 7
A Large Dun Palmer

"... with a double hook, which is of a tortuous shape in the body, obtained by tying the hooks back to back."

No. 8
A Beautiful Specimen of A Gaudy Fly

"... the body is formed in three joints. This is a famous grilse fly."

No. 9
Another Great Beauty

"... and a capital grilse or small salmon fly for any river under the sun."

No. 10
A Famous High Water Fly

"... for all salmon rivers, and is not unlike the once celebrated *Parson Fly*."

No. 11
No Name

"... a fly that will kill grilse or salmon in all rivers where the salmon and its varieties haunt."

No. 12
A Large Spring Fly

"... used generally in the Shannon, and the Tweed, when the rivers are very high and rapid."

No. 13
The Ballyshannon

"Another good killer ... a magnificent specimen ... and cannot be made properly at a small expense."

No. 14
Killarney & Tay

"Brown mohair body, with a long red-brown spotted grouse hackle; the wings of mallard, brown turkey, and a little hen pheasant tail."

No. 15
McPherson (for Spey)

"The fifteen painted salmon flies will be found great killers ... varied in size according to the state of the water."

Blacker, a famous Irish fly dresser, moved to London about 1840 and published his first book there in 1842. His *Art of Fly Making* (1855) contains beautiful hand-colored engravings of then popular patterns such as those shown here.

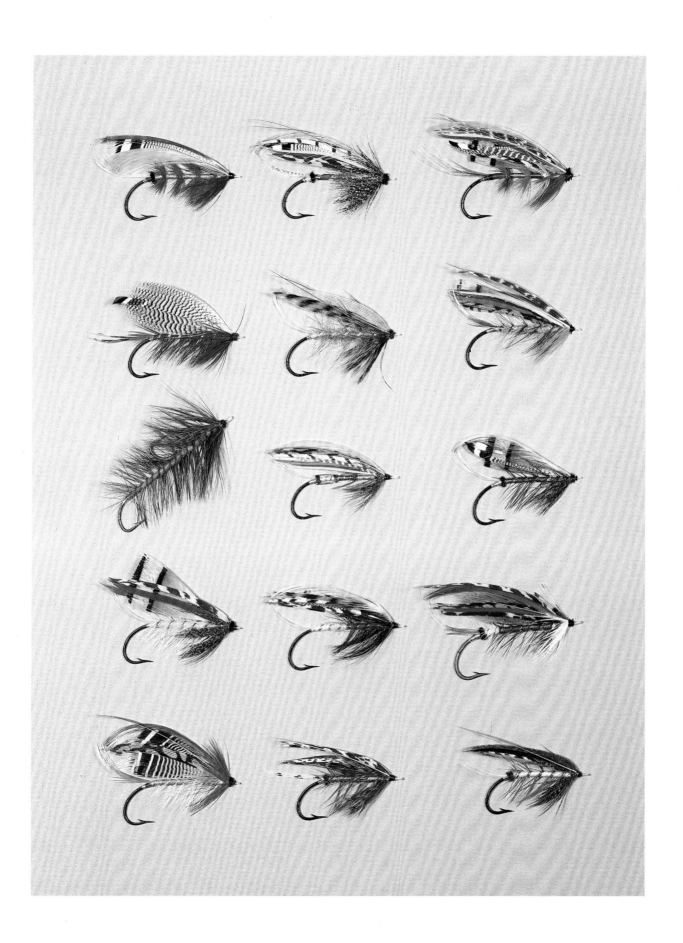

PLATE VII

The Patterns of Edward Fitzgibbon ("Ephemera")
from his *Book of the Salmon* (1847)
Dressed by Larry G. Borders, USAF

No. 1
The Goldfinch

No. 2
The Britannia

No. 3
Erin-Go-Bragh

No. 4
The Shannon

No. 5
The Dunkeld

No. 6

No. 7
Blue Jay

No. 8

No. 9

No. 10

No. 11

No. 12
The Jackass

No. 13
Ondine

No. 14

No. 15
Toppy

Evidently ignoring the tastes of the salmon, Scottish and English anglers and fly dressers admired, collected, and used exotic and brilliant patterns such as these, many of which show strong Irish influence. In some areas, however, drab patterns still held sway, such as the ever-popular *Toppy*. (These were reproduced from instructions in the book, which do not always agree with the hand-colored engravings.)

PLATE VIII

Selections from
Henry Wade's *Halcyon* (1861)

The Awe #1	*Spey Fly* #9	*Tay Fly* #11
Dee Fly #12	*Ness & Beauly* #15	*The White Swan* #18
The Pencilled Snipe #19	*The Dun Wing* #22	*Double White Top* #21
The White Top #20	*The Mottled-Wing* #28	*The Cree Fly* #31
The Canary #32	*The Doctor* #34	*The Childers* #35
The Butcher #37	*Lascelles' Golden Fly* #39	*The Butterfly* #40

Despite the influences of Irish splendor and the teachings of such experts as Blacker and Fitzgibbon, salmon flies (especially in rural areas) often remained crude and drab. But color gradually crept in, as these relatively simple midcentury patterns indicate. The advent of colorful complexity depended on location, affluence, and habit. Since published dressings like these often were ambiguous, they were subject to interpretation. Later famous classics such as the *Blue Doctor, Childers,* and *Butcher* sometimes descended from such simple ancestry.

PLATE IX

Steps in Dressing a Classic Pattern:
the *Baron*

Dressed by Ted Godfrey, Maryland

The *Baron* is a jointed-body built-wing fly similar in construction to the *Jock Scott*. Following the numbers on the opposite color plate (1) the tying thread is secured and wound to above the hook's point, where fine oval silver tinsel and ruby floss are tied in, making four turns of tinsel from a point above the barb, followed by floss wound to above the hook's point. Here, the tail (a topping) is applied and black herl for the posterior butt is tied in.

(2) The butt is wound on, and oval and flat silver tinsel wound to midway of the body, followed by oval silver ribbing. (3) The body is veiled above and below with Indian crow, and a strand of black herl is tied in for the middle butt.

Following the diagonal lower three steps downward (4) the middle butt is wound and a claret hackle, oval silver tinsel, and black floss are applied. (5) The body is wound smoothly with black floss, followed by the tinsel ribbing and the claret body hackle. These are tied off, leaving correct room for remaining ingredients. (6) Two golden pheasant tippets are mounted back to back, over which, on each side, are married strips of scarlet, blue, and yellow goose and wood duck. A jay feather for the throat is applied.

(Lower left) After winding on the throat an upper wing of strips of golden pheasant tail and peacock wing are applied and roofed with brown mallard. (Lower right) A topping of golden pheasant crest and horns of blue and yellow macaw are added, plus sides of jungle cock and cheeks of blue chatterer. The head is finished, secured by a whip-finish, and varnished to complete the fly.

Space here doesn't permit mentioning the dozens of details, tricks, and refinements necessary to dressing the *Baron* properly. Of course one must have all the materials and know how to select and prepare them for use. Correct application requires practice, study, and more practice. Some try and give up after viewing botched results. Others persevere, accepting slow progress toward the challenging goal of perfection. As this book shows, some come very close to it—masters of the complicated art of dressing the classic Atlantic salmon fly! The rewards are gems of historic beauty and the satisfaction of profound accomplishment.

PLATE X

Classic Patterns of the Aberdeenshire Dee

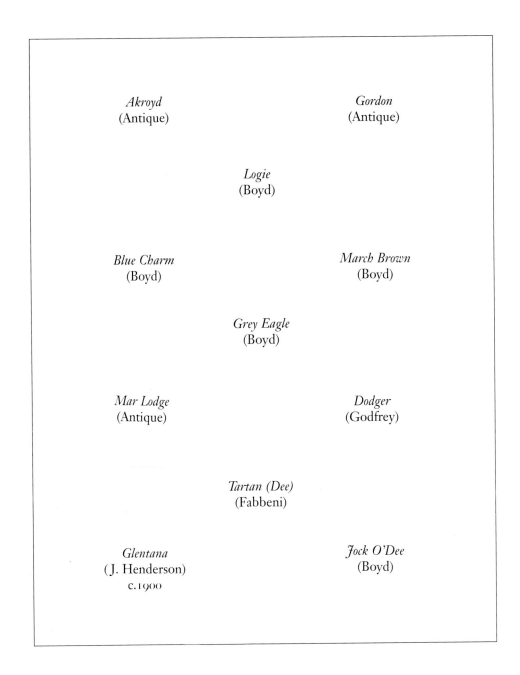

Many rivers are famous for their distinctive patterns. Traditional flies indigenous to the Aberdeenshire Dee, for example, have slim seal's-fur bodies, narrow wings of horizontal splayed turkey-wing strips, and long, flowing hackles, usually of heron. They also were noted for extra-long-shanked Limerick-bend hooks, now uncommon and difficult to obtain. Later patterns are more conventional, such as the *Mar Lodge*, originated in 1890 and named for a fishing lodge on the Upper Mar section of the Dee.

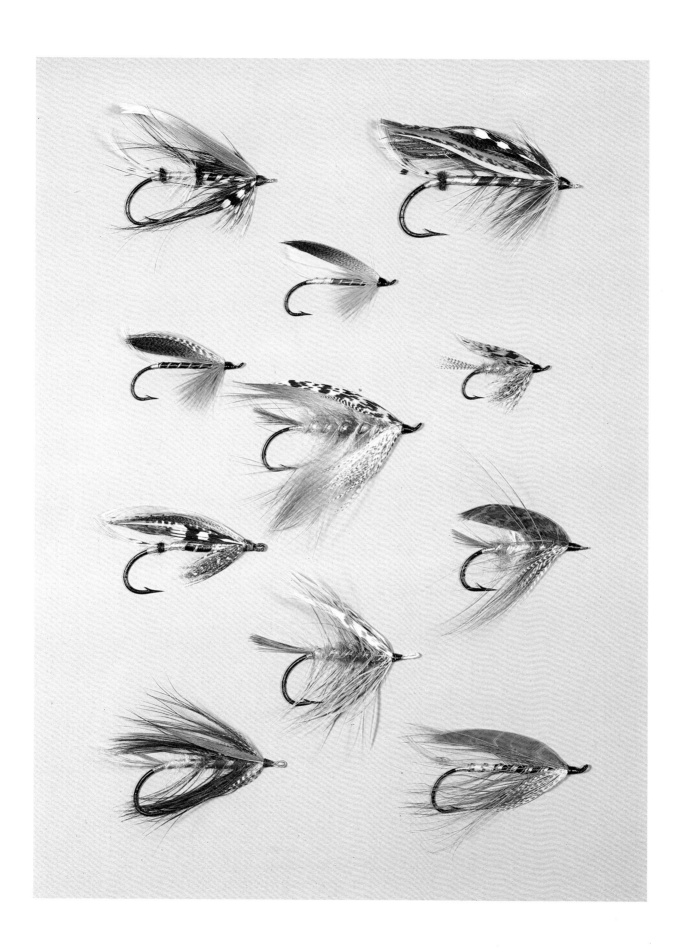

PLATE XI

Nineteenth-Century Patterns for the River Spey

Green King
(Veverka)

Lady Caroline
(Veverka)

Black Dog
(Glasso)

Black King
(Veverka)

Purple King
(Veverka)

Carron
(Veverka)

Grey Heron
(Veverka)

Gold Reeach
(Veverka)

Mrs. Grant
(Borders)

Glen Grant
(Antique)

Miss Grant
(Godfrey)

Spey flies are characterized by short, hump-backed wing strips, usually of plain brown mallard, whose natural curve enhances their drooping, and by long, mobile heron or Spey cock (now nearly extinct) body hackles tied in base first. Bodies usually are sparse, of crewels or Berlin wools, without tags, tails, or butts. There may be several ribbings, of gold and/or silver tinsels, or threads. One is usually wound in reverse to hold the body hackle in place. The three lower patterns honor members of the Grant family, of Castle Grant, on middle Spey.

PLATE XII

Old Favorites for Welsh Rivers

The Llanover
Francis' pattern
(Fabbeni)

Bittern
Francis' pattern
(Fabbeni)

Francis' Favourite
Francis' pattern
(Fabbeni)

Berrington's Favourite
Francis' pattern
(Fabbeni)

Berrington's USK Fairy
Francis' pattern
(Fabbeni)

Berrington's Orange
Francis' pattern
(Fabbeni)

Wye Grub
Pryce–Tannatt's pattern
(Fabbeni)

The Captain
Kelson's pattern
(Godfrey)

USK Grub
Farlow's pattern
(Fabbeni)

No. 4, Conway River Series
Francis' pattern
(Fabbeni)

Dai Benn
Eric Coombs' pattern
(Fabbeni)

Fairy Queen
Kelson's pattern
(Borders)

The Blackwall
Blackwall's pattern
(Fabbeni)

Trewern Tickler
Benyon's pattern
(Fabbeni)

Gamekeeper
Francis' pattern
(Antique)

Despite the proximity of Wales to Ireland, Welsh patterns remained sober in color and few in number to the mid-1800s (see Plate III). Then, with the influence of visiting anglers such as Francis Francis, more color and variety were introduced, as the adjoining plate shows. On the more sequestered rivers, however, the older drab patterns continued popular, gradually giving way, to an extent, to the brighter and fancier classics.

PLATE XIII

Francis Francis' General Patterns
from his *A Book on Angling* (1867)

Dressed by Larry G. Borders, USAF

The Highlander   *The Doctor*

The Indian Crow

The Claret   *The Blue Ranger*

The Shannon

The Spider   *The Baker*

The Nicholson

The Crane   *The Dhoon Fly*

Francis Francis (1822–1886) contributed greatly to the popularity of the classics by publishing his book (in at least six editions) featuring fifty-two named and many un-named salmon flies. These (from his sixth edition) show typical examples then in vogue. His *Shannon* (there are several) calls for "two bright yellow macaw feathers with black streak down the center," feathers he admits were "not easy to obtain" and which have been substituted for here.

PLATE XIV

Patterns from
George M. Kelson's *The Salmon Fly* (1895)

Dressed by Albert J. Cohen, Texas

Blue Doctor

Dawson   Golden Drop

Gordon

Infallible   John Ferguson

Napoleon

Queen of Autumn   Sir Richard

Una

Kelson originated his complex version of the mixed wing by marrying a few differently colored wing fibers together and then repeating this sequence several times; one married group joining another, to form a sheath of the desired width for the outer wing (or "skin") of the fly. An identical but opposite assembly was made for the other side of the wing. Shorter fibers were used nearest the body, gradually lengthening to the crest. These two sheaths then were "humped" for proper curvature before mounting. This is illustrated by the ten masterfully dressed patterns on this plate. Kelson's mixed wing was unsuited to flies of other characters and often was simplified.

(first of two plates)

PLATE XV

Patterns from
George M. Kelson's *The Salmon Fly* (1895)

Juno	*Gitana*	*Quinchat*
Black Prince	*Golden Butterfly* (Waslick)	*Ghost* (Malloch)
Chatterer	*Popham* (Kelson)	*Harlequin*
Barkworth	*Gordon Cumming*	*Heather Dog*
Excelsior	*Lady Bell*	*Trahern's Wonder*

The three patterns in the top row are from Kelson's articles in *The Fishing Gazette* (1884). The *Golden Butterfly* shown here is Kelson's pattern, not Pat McKay's original described on page 38. The *Ghost* pattern is an antique dressed by P. D. Malloch, of Scotland. The *Popham* is documented as having been dressed by Kelson, himself. All flies on this plate except the three noted above were dressed by Ted Godfrey, Maryland.

(second of two plates)

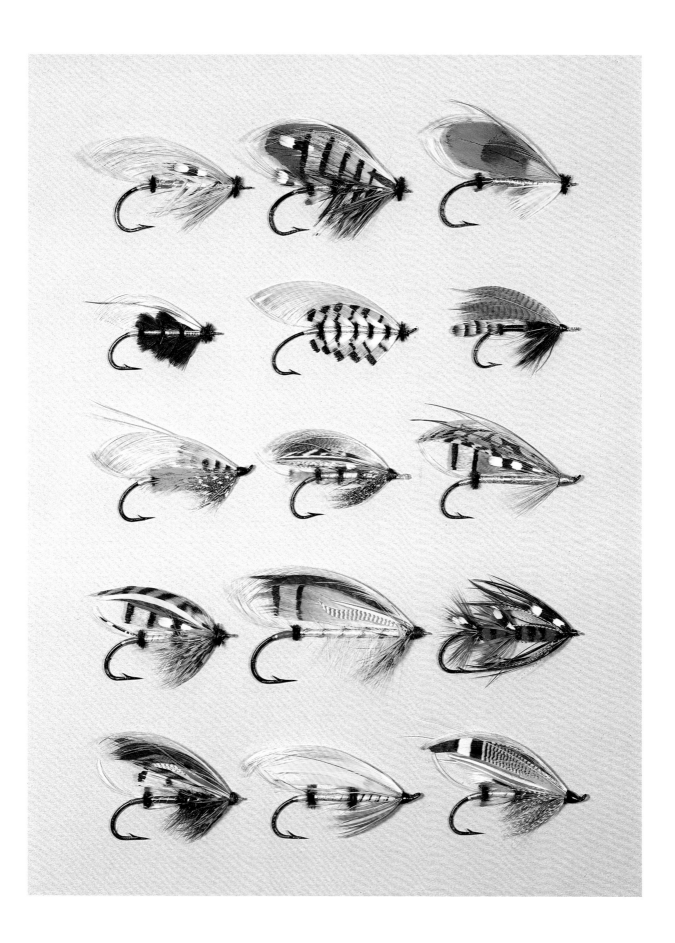

PLATE XVI

Patterns from Sir Herbert Maxwell's
Salmon and Sea Trout (1898)
and *Fishing at Home and Abroad* (1913)

Argus
(Borders)

The Sun Fly
(Borders)

Rory
(Borders)

Hell Fire
(Borders)

Silver Secretary
(Borders)

Wormald
(Borders)

Yellow Eagle
(Antique, c.1900)

Snow Fly
(Hardy Bros., c.1900)

Even though Sir Herbert Maxwell favored simple flies and considered complicated classics unnecessary, he admired fancy patterns and illustrated many, such as those shown here, in his books. Large flies like these could easily be "thrown" to surprising distances with two-handed rods about 17 feet long. This was popular and efficient tackle for big rivers in high-water seasons.

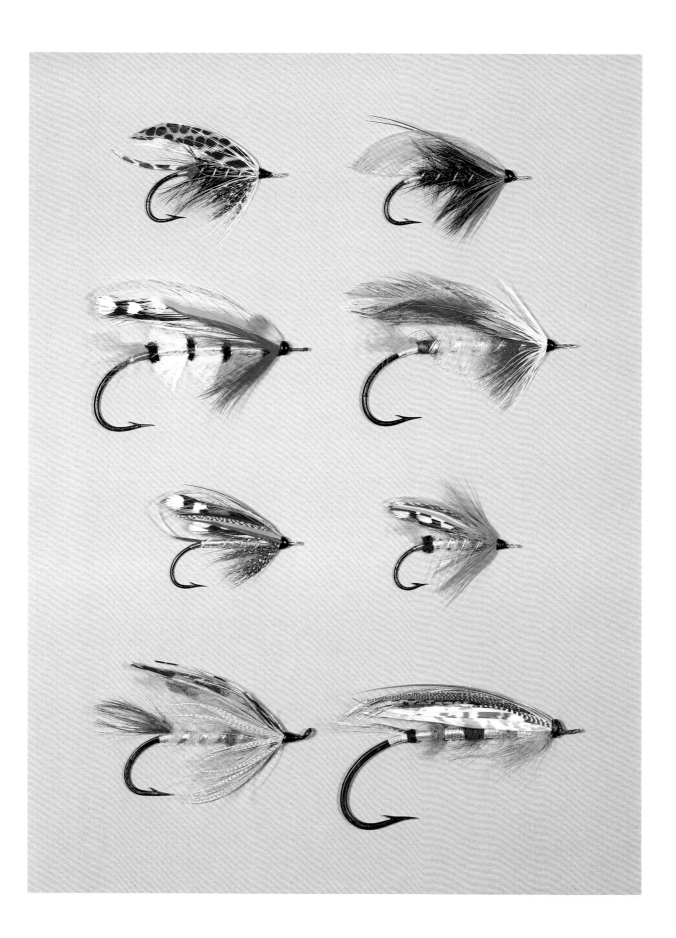

PLATE XVII

Patterns from John James Hardy's
Salmon Fishing (1907)
Dressed by Ronald K. Alcott, Massachusetts

Murdoch	*Bonne Bouche*	*Brown Dog*

McIntyre	*Red Drummond*

Charlie	*Parson*	*Sir Richard Sutton*

Butcher	*Red Sandy*	*Wilkinson*

John J. Hardy was a partner in the British firm of Hardy Brothers. His book treats salmon-fishing tackle and methods and contains chapters on salmon flies and a dressing "lesson." Its main value is in the abbreviated formulas for identifying 344 prominent classic patterns as discussed in Chapter Ten. Some of the flies popular at the turn of the century are illustrated on the accompanying color plate.

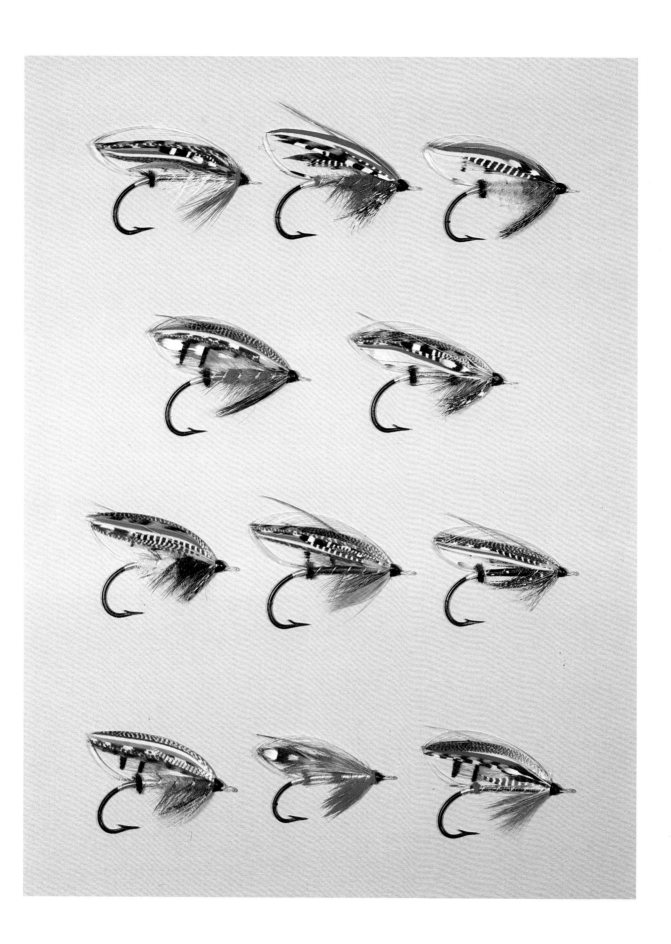

PLATE XVIII

Selections from Dr. T. E. Pryce–Tannatt's
How to Dress Salmon Flies (1914)

Black Prince
(Boyd)

Dreadnought
(Boyd)

Durham Ranger
(Antique)

Blue Limerick
(Boyd)

Evening Star
Pryce–Tannatt's pattern
(Hibbitts)

Canary
(Borders)

Green Peacock
(Borders)

Childers
(Boyd)

Alexandra
(Borders)

Helmsdale
(Boyd)

Claret Alder
(low-water pattern)
(Glasso)

Thunder & Lightning
(Alcott)

Candlestick Maker
(Boyd)

Blue & Yellow Wasp
(Borders)

Dandy
(Godfrey)

Grouse & Orange
(Borders)

Brown Shrimp
(Younger)

Contrary to Kelson's complexity, Dr. Pryce–Tannatt was a practical and expert angler and fly dresser who gained beautiful results while simplifying patterns made intricate by others. For example he made Kelson's mixed (or compound) wing easier by using "strands" of thin strips of various wing colors married together instead of the more laborious method described beside Plate XIV.

(first of two plates)

PLATE XIX

Selections from Dr. T. E. Pryce–Tannatt's
How to Dress Salmon Flies (1914)

Spring Grub
(Borders)

White Wing
(Borders)

Silver Wilkinson
(Malloch)

Jock Scott
(Alcott)

Claret Alder
(Alcott)

Green Highlander
(Alcott)

Rosy Dawn
(Alcott)

Torrish
(Alcott)

Variegated Sun Fly
(Borders)

Sherbrook
(Alcott)

Tippet Grub
(Jorgensen)

Joe Brady
(Borders)

Teal & Red
(Borders)

Dr. Pryce–Tannatt's book provides 100 choice and detailed classic dressings prominent around the turn of the century, such as those shown here. The book also offers expert instruction on dressing important fly types and is embellished with eight superb color plates of classic patterns. It is a key volume for those interested in this subject.

(second of two plates)

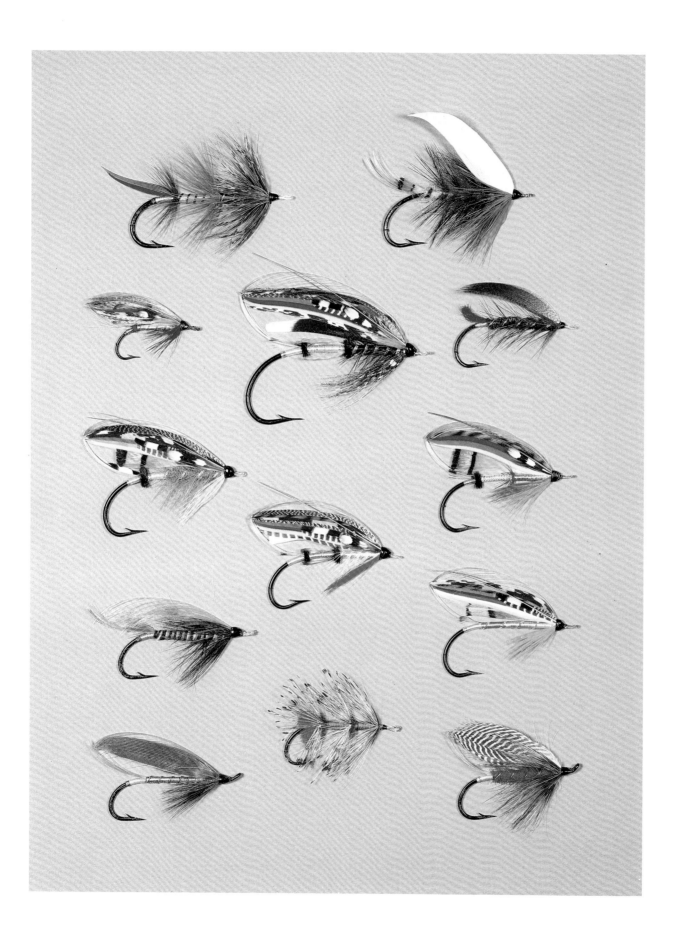

PLATE XX

Early North-American Feather-Wing Patterns

Mitchell
(Bean)

Lanctot
(Godfrey)

Night Hawk
(Bean)

Wilmot
(MacPherson)

Lady Amherst
(Wm. Mills & Son)
(repaired after use)

Nicholson
(Godfrey)

Grey Fly
(Godfrey)

Forsyth
(Godfrey)

Ross
(Godfrey)

Louise
(Godfrey)

Notion
(Godfrey)

Stephens
(Godfrey)

Strachan
(Godfrey)

Parson
(Godfrey)

Chamberlain
(Godfrey)

While American and Canadian anglers used British classics extensively, they also originated many patterns of their own in the decades around the turn of the century. It is
natural for some of these to indicate British antecedents. The *Mitchell, Night Hawk,*
and *Lady Amherst* are enduringly popular American classics. Further information is
found in the books by Norris, Roosevelt, and Sage listed in the bibliography herewith.

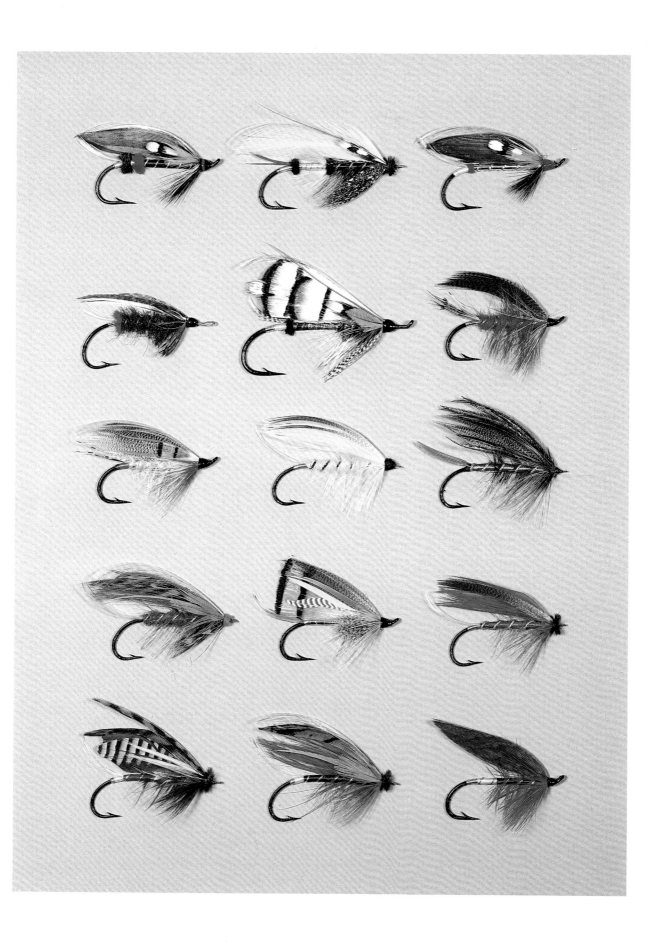

PLATE XXI

Modern North-American Salmon Flies

Thunder & Lightning
Hair-wing version
(Ent)

Green Highlander
Hair-wing version
(Bigaouette)

Jock Scott
Hair-wing version
(Ent)

Blue Doctor
Hair-wing version
(Author)

Black Dose
Hair-wing version
(Alcott)

Muddler Minnow
(Gapen)

Black Bear (Green Butt)
(Alcott)

Red Abbey
c.1915

Ringer
(Westfall)

Orange Blossom
(Bigaouette)

Rusty Rat
(Newcomb)

Silver Rat
(Newcomb)

Cosseboom
(Author)

Herb Johnson Special
(Johnson)

Colburn (Green)
(Ent)

With this century's decline of the classics and advent of simpler hair-wing patterns, almost a complete change occurred internationally in salmon flies used for fishing. Since this transition is necessary in completing our account, this and the next two color plates outline it. The first five flies at the top here indicate that the change included adapting some of the classics to hair-wing variations.

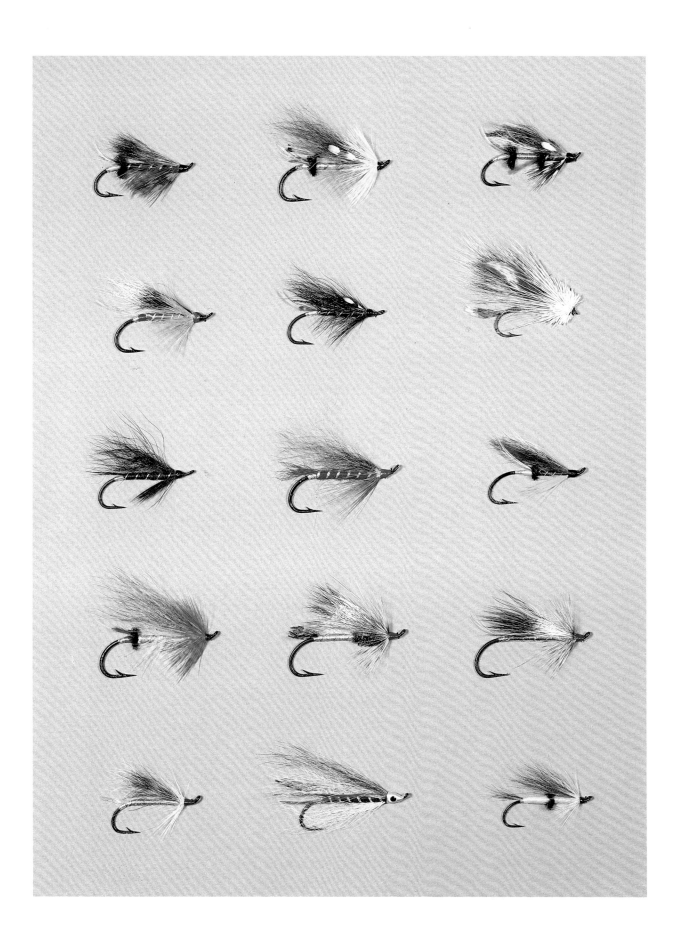

PLATE XXII

Low-Water Patterns and Nymphs for Salmon

Green Highlander   Jock Scott   Durham Ranger   Silver Grey

Blue Charm   Black Jack   Night Hawk   Royal Coachman

Cosseboom

Gold Salmon Nymph
(DeFeo)

Black Salmon Nymph
(DeFeo)

Red Creeper

March Brown   Brown Creeper   Copper Creeper
(Niemeyer)

Red Quill   Brown Quill   Jay Quill   Ginger Quill
(Niemeyer)   (Niemeyer)   (Niemeyer)   (Niemeyer)

This plate shows two important types for summer fishing. Low-water patterns are smaller-sized flies tied on larger irons for better hooking ability, as the top nine illustrate. Classics often are dressed this way when small flies for thin waters seem necessary. Since salmon strike at nymphs, the lower ten are included. They also presumably take low-wing, wingless, or bedraggled patterns for nymphs or grubs. Several classics such as the *Spring Grub* and *Tippet Grub* imitate these.

PLATE XXIII

Modern Patterns for Iceland and Continental Europe

Blue Charm
(Miller)

Sweep
(Arnason)

Irish Hairy Mary
(Boyd)

Crosfield
(Martinez)

Blue Rat
(Martinez)

Krafla (Red)
(Gislasson)

Birna
(Arnason)

Raekja
(Gislasson)

Francis (Red)
(Deane)

General Practitioner
(Drury)

Namsen, No. 1
(Mustad)
Norway

Namsen, No. 2
(Sand)
Norway

Namsen, No. 3
(Olsen)
Norway

Peer Gynt
(Sand)
Norway

Bretonne
(Mouches-Ragot)
France

Gave
(Mouches-Ragot)
France

Allier
(Mouches-Ragot)
France

Silver Orange
(Martinez)
Spain

Pas River
(Martinez)
Spain

Navia River
(Martinez)
Spain

Icelandic favorites include the upper ten shown here, plus tube flies and Sheep patterns. Orange patterns may be taken for prawns or shrimps, while bucktail types evidently simulate elvers or baitfish. Similar designs are popular in Scandinavian countries, which also have native patterns, seen in the next row. French patterns are usually as plain as the early and sober British ones. Spanish anglers often prefer classics and similarly ornate moderns like the three Martinez originals on the bottom row.

PLATE XXIV

Presentation and Exhibition Patterns

Columbia
Designed by author
(Alcott)

Colonel Bates
(Boyd)

The Colonel's Lady
(Designed & dressed by
Alcott)

Eve's Fancy
(Fabbeni)

Evening Star
Hale's pattern
(Alcott)

Aglaia
(Borders)

Sutherland
(Boyd)

Brora
(Boyd)

Opera
(Designed & dressed by
Boyd)

Covent Garden
(Designed & dressed by
Boyd)

Countess of Seafield
(Boyd)

Rocke's Fancy
(Godfrey)

Duchess
(Alcott)

Sir Herbert
Pryce–Tannatt's pattern
(Fabbeni)

The decline of classic patterns for fishing prompted their enthusiastic rebirth as crowning challenges for fly dressers and as beautiful and historic gems for collectors. These intricate Victorian designs were deemed too precious to be forgotten. Exquisite workmanship, choicest ingredients, and faithful reproduction constitute hallmarks of the modern collector's items. Original patterns also are designed to honor persons or to commemorate events.

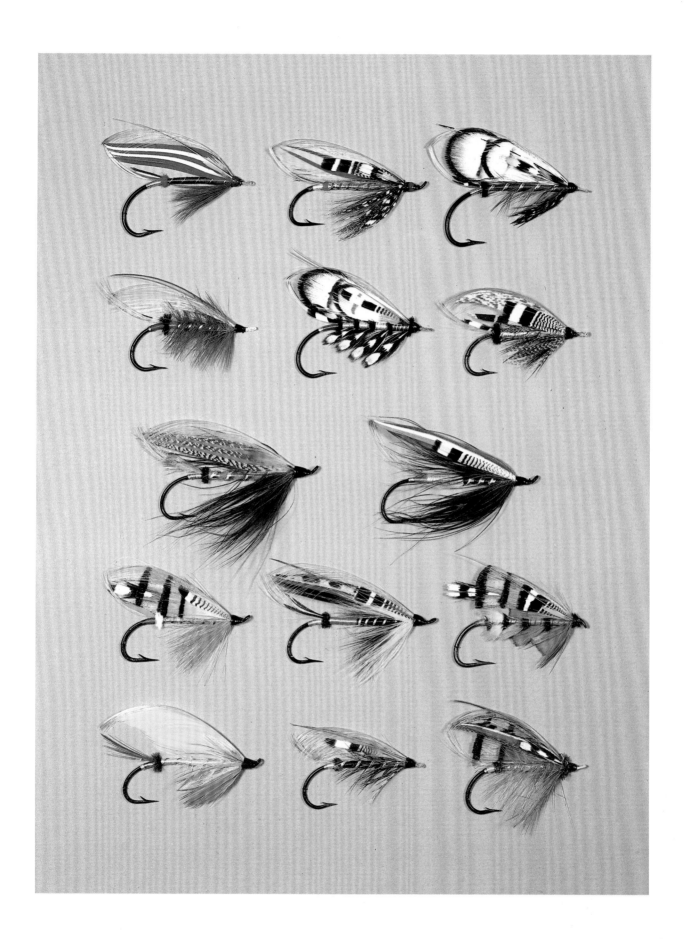

PLATE XXV

The Best Time of Day, by Henry McDaniel

for dressing 240 patterns, which seem as correct as such can be. Readers who desire to assemble classic-salmon-fly collections would take a giant step by concentrating on acquiring the patterns Kelson describes.

In 1892 an English army officer who signed himself as "Captain Hale" published a valuable guide called *How to Tie Salmon Flies*. The captain stayed purely within his subject. His directions were so clear that his book is essential to students of the art as it was practiced. Although it predates Kelson's work by three years, Kelson was the earlier writer because he was steadily published in *The Fishing Gazette* as early as 1884. Hale credits Kelson with about half of his forty patterns, evidently obtained from these articles. Others are credited to authorities such as Peter Malloch, of Perth, and William Brown, of Aberdeen.

During a time when most anglers preferred gut eyes on their hooks, Hale was sensible enough to favor metal ones, saying they last longer, keep better, are more dependable, save the fly dresser's time, make the bodies slimmer, and the heads smaller. His advice on materials in vogue then is historical and practical. Hackles and methods of dying them are exhaustively treated. He considers sun the enemy of natural or dyed feathers or furs and, to avoid fading, recommends against exposing flies in one's hat (or clipped to a vest, I might add).

In perusing Hale's book for beautiful and unusual patterns we note that his *Evening Star*, with four graduated double jungle cock veilings above and below, is entirely different from the one given by Pryce–Tannatt, which has three graduated pairs of jungle cock and several toppings in the wing. Both are worthy gems for any collection. Pryce–Tannatt's is illustrated on Plate XVIII. Hale credits his to Kelson, but it doesn't appear in Kelson's book. Since it seems far too lovely to fish with it is included with the exhibition patterns on Plate XXIV. Here are both dressings:

Evening Star

PRYCE–TANNATT

Tag	Silver thread and lemon floss	*Throat*	A deep-blue hackle, quite full
Tail	A topping	*Wing*	Three pairs of jungle cock feathers (back to back), each pair shorter than the preceding; four or five toppings over
Body	Black seal's fur (picked out toward the shoulder)		
Ribbing	Oval silver tinsel		
Hackle	A black hackle, from tail		

Evening Star

HALE

Tag Silver twist and tippet colored silk

Tail A topping

Butt Black herl

Body In four equal sections: the first three of silver tinsel, each having two jungle cock back to back above and below, and each butted with black herl; the last division of blue floss, the only one ribbed with silver tinsel, oval

Throat Jungle cock as before. These and the body veilings each slightly increase in length from the rear end of the body

Wing Four Amherst pheasant tippets in two pairs back to back, the outer pair shorter than the inner pair; a topping over

Cheeks On each side, the tip of a barred summer duck feather and a shorter Indian crow feather

Horns Red macaw

Head Black herl

Many of the spectacular flies described in Kelson's book are what he calls "exaggerations" (what we call "vanity" or "exhibition" patterns), an appellation he gives to too few. Nevertheless we thank him for including them. Many of the others were, and are, successful salmon enticers for those who wish to use them.

When collectors acquire sets of antique flies they usually find the inventories to include so many of the same patterns that, sight unseen, they can guess what they will be. They usually include the Doctors (Blue, Silver, and/or Black), *Dusty Miller, Green Highlander, Jock Scott, Mar Lodge, Silver Grey,* and *Thunder & Lightning,* but rarely the more unusual specimens. For the unusual ones collectors must sharpen their detective instincts or settle for modern counterparts. And these modern examples can be of better workmanship and more attractive than the antiques.

There are several reasons why these six ornate patterns are described in this chapter. Some are not found in other books and should be perpetuated. All are surpassingly handsome, offering the supreme challenge to fly dressers and exotic appeal to collectors. They illustrate the complexity of detail and the extravagance of rare feathers inherent in so many patterns of Victorian times. They typify the extreme development, which sensible anglers greeted critically around the turn of the twentieth century.

The nineteenth century's beginning saw the classic salmon fly burst from its primitive bud. Its middle and ending saw it bloom into full flower, providing a heritage of historic beauty surpassing anything in the annals of angling. But the blossom's cloying fragrance began to pall. Too much was enough!

Thus, as we will soon see, the importance of the classic salmon fly separates into two important parts. One concerns its value to fishing, which has gradually diminished yet will probably never completely die. We cling to the charm of the handcrafted split-bamboo rod despite the greater practicality of synthetic fibers, and there always will be some nostalgic anglers who consider only exquisite classic salmon flies suitable for the King of Fishes. Using commoner tempters would decrease the fun.

The second direction of the classic flies' history relates to the salmon fly as an entrancing art form, and those who consider it less than that simply fail to understand its many complicated facets. As I write this I am mindful of other lures usually grouped as "flies" made by hand to tempt sport fish, and I remember the truly great artists who excel in such specialties in one form or another: George Grant, with his lifelike woven-hair masterpieces; Robert Veverka, with his graceful streamer flies; Ted Niemeyer, with his buglike nymphs that can almost crawl; Lee Wulff and Harry Darbee, with their delicate dry flies for salmon and trout; and others too numerous to mention.

But even these experts, when they view the vivid complexity of classic salmon flies by artists like Ronald Alcott and Larry Borders, must feel a tinge of envy. Call me biased if you wish, but even a glance at the color plates of this book should suggest the possibilities and the range of the salmon fly. Kelson missed an important point in his book. He was writing about a cherished period in angling history, but he didn't realize it at the time. He wasn't really writing entirely about practical patterns for hooking salmon, even though he maintained that he was. Rather, he was writing about an esthetic, a path to beauty.

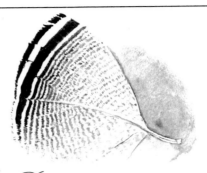

CHAPTER NINE

Dissension

$\mathcal{E}$LABORATE nonsense, scoffed one critic, contemptuously snubbing the complicated classics. He was joined by a growing band of adherents as the nineteenth century drew to a close. Simpler patterns were again in vogue. This return to simplicity may not have been entirely a reaction to Kelson's extravagances, but he was as responsible as any for the movement away from exaggerated and complex patterns.

In addition to their fancy tails, compound bodies with multiple veilings, and multicolored mixed wings, Kelson's flies show that their maker was imbued with a taste for the rarest feathers. For example he claims credit for the patterns *Highland Gem, Ike Dean,* and *Silver Ardea.* The first two are butted with feathers of the golden bird of paradise, and the latter specifies it in its tail.

Wondering why Kelson thought he had to send to the southwestern Pacific for rare feathers to tempt salmon, I researched this bird in Cooper and Forshaw's authoritative and elegantly illustrated elephant folio *The Birds of Paradise and Bower Birds* (1977 and 1979). I found no bird of this name and no reference to the Latin name Kelson gives for it. He does say that he favors its brilliant yellow neck hackles, which he considers superior to toucan or macaw. He may have meant the flamed bower bird, but this is no matter except that it illustrates the following point.

Why all the fuss over scarce feathers when dyed fowl hackles would do just as well? Why all this complexity when simpler patterns were more sensible? To understand this we must psychoanalyze anglers of the late nineteenth century. They were mostly aristocrats (or people who aped them) who were used to the very best and to whom needless extravagance meant very little. If imported natural feathers were considered superior to dyed domestic ones, anglers (and therefore fly dressers) would search the earth for them. If complicated patterns were considered more desirable than simpler ones, they were status symbols which seemed essential for that reason alone. Anglers had to be pleased if fly dressers were to stay in business. Never mind about pleasing the salmon: under favorable conditions they would strike at most anything, anyway!

Money was no object to rich gentleman anglers in the pre-income-tax days of vast fortunes and huge landed estates. But nearing the end of the century Victorian extravagance became increasingly burdensome. The great British estates, for example, began to disappear, and even such small things as fishing flies drifted toward economy and simplicity. Then, too, there seemed to be a change in thinking, a reaction against past excessive action. Sensible anglers gazed lovingly at these overdressed confections of fancy furs and feathers and started to wonder if things weren't being carried a bit too far.

One discerning angler who thought things were being carried too far is our old friend, one of the habitués of the Three Salmons Hotel, Sir Herbert Maxwell, author of several angling books including *Salmon and Sea Trout* (1898). He remarked, "It is an extraordinary delusion that every river requires its peculiar combination of silk, wool, tinsel and feathers to take the salmon which frequent it. Thus, we have Tweed flies, Tay flies, Spey flies, Usk flies, Shannon flies, none of which it is orthodox to use on any stream except that from whence it derived its origin."

He notes that Francis' book contains over a hundred different rivers for which they are held appropriate, if not essential, and that it also gives a list of seventeen "general" flies recommended for use anywhere. Maxwell remarks: "In the whole range of angling there is no subject upon which such irreconcilable differences of opinion prevail as upon the need for variety in salmon flies and the respective merits of different patterns."

The author sums up: "It does not matter what is the colour or material of the object called a salmon fly that one presents to the notice of a salmon, provided that it is not too large to excite suspicion, or too small to escape observation, and that it is given a lifelike motion."

Maxwell remarks the shift from early-century drab bucolic patterns to late-century gaudy and complicated ones, saying, "Where are the old-fashioned sober hued flies like *Toppy*, *White Tip* and *Dun Wing*, once reputed indispensable to the Tweed angler? Bright flies are all the rage just now; *Durham Ranger*, *Dandy*, *Wilkinson* and *Silver Grey* are prime favourites at present."

Francis, in 1886, naively writes, "The fish have undergone a complete change in their tastes since I was there [on Tweed]; for when I was there they preferred a sober-coloured fly, but of late years they prefer more showy ones."

Did Francis really think it was salmon that had changed tastes, or did he understand that it was the anglers who had come to favor gaudy patterns as devotedly as their grandfathers had spurned them?

Maxwell settles the question:

> The conclusion is that I would feel as confident of success with the old type of fly as with the new, or vice versa. The unromantic conclusion to which observant anglers have come is that the colour and materials of a fly matter very little, if anything, while the size and movement thereof is all important.

I'll go along with Maxwell only part way. I think selecting the relative brightness of a fly to suit weather and water conditions *does* make a difference. But further refinement is mere window dressing. Tying, selecting, using, and discussing salmon flies is fun, however, and variety is the spice of life! Choosing the proper fly to fish with is too often guided by superstition, such as the guide's recommendation, or which one was most successful yesterday.

Maxwell believed that salmon couldn't distinguish colors very well, especially when the fly was between the fish and the sun. He evidently considered three types sufficient; light (tints), dark (blackish), and bright (perhaps well tinseled), and he thought it most important to have them in a variety of sizes. Thus, he deemed the wide variety of complex patterns then in vogue ludicrous and unnecessary, but he loved them nevertheless, as shown by some of his favorites on Plate XVI. There must have been some hot arguments at the Three Salmons Hotel when Maxwell aired his opinions with Kelson and Francis perhaps listening in. But probably he tactfully muffled his criticism under such circumstances.

Maxwell, despite his dissent over the plethora of patterns then in vogue, gives the dressing of fifty in his *Salmon and Sea Trout* (1898). Some of these are the well-known classics, but others are uncommon and of special interest, as the examples on Plate XVI indicate. Since the one named for him is one of the few with a gold body, it may be of interest to give it here:

Tag and Body	All one, of gold tinsel, ribbed with gold twist	*Wing*	Two tippet feathers, rather long, a pair of shorter jungle cock over, with strips of gold pheasant tail and white and scarlet dyed swan, and a good slice of wood duck. A few fibers of emerald peacock herl; topping over, blue chatterer cheeks, red macaw horns
Tail	A topping and Indian crow		
Hackle	Dyed golden cock's down the body. One fourth of the body next the shoulder is of scarlet mohair, picked out, over which a crimson cock's hackle for shoulder		
		Head	Black or green chenille

Probably the foremost dissenter who preferred Puritan simplicity to Victorian complexity was a dedicated British salmon angler named A. H. Chaytor, who wrote *Letters to a Salmon Fisher's Sons* in 1910 about angling experiences a few years earlier. This book of diary excerpts in letter form contains valuable angling wisdom on salmon-fishing tactics and fishing flies. Chaytor's is a practical book stressing his opinion that decorations on salmon flies that have "no fishing value" are useless, a position quite opposite from that we have been discussing.

Nevertheless Chaytor makes a strong case that simplicity, as well as ornateness, can be an art form, and he illustrates this by describing three of his patterns, which follow. Ordinarily tags, tails, horns, butts, and similar fripperies are eliminated. Winging is simplified, and throat hackling is reduced to between one and two turns. Obviously Chaytor lacked his predecessors' superstitious reverence for the complicated patterns. Considering them beautiful and fascinating, acknowledging they provided practice and pleasure for fly dressers, he concluded that for the true purpose of angling, the simpler and more lightly dressed patterns served just as well or better.

Disgusted with commercial overdressed flies made to please anglers who assumed if a little dressing was good, a lot was better, Chaytor has this to say:

Many of the costly shop flies are so overloaded with feathers that when in the water they are only a sodden lump and all life and movement is destroyed. These flies only begin to kill fish when they get old and knocked to bits with use. Their confiding owner usually has a giant [fly] book full of similar glories and he spends a large part of his time, when he ought to be fishing, in inspecting these flies to decide which he shall use next, and then tying it on in place of the one he has last preferred.

This is a modern problem as well as an older one, an excellent reason for learning to dress one's own flies (to which I might add again that one of the peaks of angling pleasure is to hook a fish on a fly tied by your own hand). The point also is well taken that we change flies too often, ignoring the fact that we can never expect results if our fly is out of the water. I think it was A. H. E. Wood, the expert angler of Cairnton, who said he would be willing to fish all season through with a *March Brown* and that he could hook as many fish with it as with frequently changed patterns. Probably anyone could, especially if he had a variety of sizes!

Chaytor continues, on the same subject:

But I do not wish to sneer at the possessor of many flies. There are plenty of keen fishers to whom the making or collecting of workmanlike flies is in itself a labour of love, but I think it is generally true that the better the fisher and the greater his opportunities of fishing, the fewer are the flies that you shall find him using; certainly it is so with the most skillful fishers I have known.

Here are three of Chaytor's simple patterns. They are quick and easy to dress and very pretty when correctly proportioned. They should not be neglected.

White & Silver

Body Oval silver tinsel	*Wing* Dark turkey
Hackle A rather long white hackle	*Cheeks* Jungle cock
(not more than two turns)	

This fly has no tail, tag, butt, or any other adornment. Sometimes a light-blue hackle is substituted, which may be of advantage in Iceland. Despite Chaytor's opinion I like this and many other flies with a tail of a well-shaped topping, a dressing element which seems to be of advantage because it is filled with light and sparkle, moving up and down in currents or while being fished. The above pattern sometimes is called *Silver & White*.

─────────────────── *Claret Fly* ───────────────────

Body	Rough claret wool or seal's fur	*Wing*	Bronze mallard, or brown turkey tail, usually set horizontally
Ribbing	Broad silver tinsel		
Hackle	Claret		

─────────────────── *Gipps* ───────────────────

Body	Half black and then orange-brown seal's fur	*Hackle*	Black
Ribbing	Narrow tinsel	*Wing*	Dun turkey tail strips

──

The first two patterns were designed for high to normal water and are dressed on appropriately large hooks. The third pattern is recommended for low, clear water. All hackling is very sparse.

For every dissident whose opinions were published, there were many who also favored the simpler patterns but whose opinions went unrecorded. Another who *was* published, although not very much, was Ernest M. Crosfield, an Englishman reputed to have been the greatest salmon-fly dresser of the decades straddling the turn of the century.

Let's get acquainted with Crosfield's philosophy by quoting the gist of an article on tying salmon flies which he wrote under the pen name of Poacher. It was published in the January 7th, 1923 issue of *Salmon & Trout* magazine. The author says:

When fishing in spring the pattern of fly, or method of tying, does not matter much. Size is the main thing. In summer salmon are much more particular, and this is a time when the usual type of shop-dressed fly fails. The ordinary fly tyer uses far too much material. Consequently the fly, instead of being thin and transparent, is more or less opaque when held up to light.

The blame rests mainly on the fisherman who, instead of holding a fly up to the light and looking at it as a salmon would do, judges it by its appearance as seen from above. Nor will the average fisherman believe that quite small, thin and lightly dressed flies must be used if one wants to catch salmon in low, clear water in summer.

The salmon is not necessarily attracted by all the fancy feathers and complicated dressings which are so pleasing to the eye of inexperienced fishermen. Flies plainly dressed with a few inexpensive materials would probably kill just as well, or even possibly better, than most of the modern fancy patterns. Our forefathers, who probably caught as many salmon as we do, used quite plain looking flies. Tying some of the modern patterns is a difficult and complicated business. I am convinced that the trouble involved is quite unnecessary, as far as catching salmon is concerned.

Crosfield's flies had three characteristics that should be valuable to modern fly dressers and anglers. They featured *economy of material*—no more than necessary to do the job, and everything used, in part at least, being required to show. He believed that every element should have a purpose and fulfill it, or should not be used.

Crosfield's flies featured *intentional translucence* in their wings, reminiscent of Michael Rogan's. Crosfield tied fibers on in bunches rather than all together, such as a few fibers of tippet and perhaps a few of something else tied in as a bunch on one side of the hook and the same on the other, perhaps repeating this double-bunching before applying the topping or roof. The throat often was wound on between these applications and was composed of not more than two turns of hackle. As a result, every fiber stood out, separated from all the others, to provide maximum light reflection and action.

Crosfield's patterns also featured *slimness of dressing*. He preferred iron-eyed hooks at a time when gut-eyes were more popular, because slimmer bodies could be dressed on them. He used no more materials than necessary in order to obtain maximum translucency. His bodies did not extend beyond the point of the barb, on the theory that this would make salmon take the hook better.

Regardless of these simplifications, Crosfield seemed to straddle between the two extremes of Victorian "elaborate nonsense" and Puritan simplicity. This may make more sense than to have gone to either extreme, and certainly his known patterns combine both beauty and practicality. His most famous one is the *Black Silk*, a fly well worth a modern swim on the tackle of those who cling to tradition without excessive frills. Crosfield says of it, "This is a very favourite pattern of mine, and with it I have caught fish in many rivers and in all heights and conditions of water, of course varying the size to suit the conditions. I look upon this pattern and the *Thunder & Lightning* as two of the best dark flies." Here is Crosfield's pattern the way he gave it:

Black Silk

Tag	Silver twist and yellow floss	*Throat hackle*	Blue jay
Tail	A topping with a few strands (fibers) of tippet	*Over-wing*	About six strands from a golden pheasant's tail and about two strands from Amherst pheasant's tail, to be tied on together on left side, and the same again on the right side. Two narrow strips of dark mallard, one on top of the other, to be tied on together on the top as a covering for the whole wing
Body	Black silk (floss) ribbed with oval silver tinsel		
Body hackle	Bright claret		
Under-wing	Tippet strands, the point of golden pheasant breast feather and one or two toppings. Each feather to be tied on separately so as to keep the wing as open and transparent as possible		

I notice in Eric Taverner's important books *Fly Tying for Salmon* (1942) and *Salmon Fishing* (1948) that illustrations of this fly as dressed by Crosfield show a narrow strip of barred wood duck on each side directly under the mallard, evidently instead of the Amherst pheasant tail.

Crosfield provides a tip on applying mallard as a roofing: "A *single* strip of mallard is one of the most difficult feathers to tie neatly on the wing, but if two narrow strips are placed one on top of the other before putting in position to tie in, they 'sit' without any difficulty." Such a strip would be snipped from the feather; the strip would be "squared" and folded over. Crosfield says, "Let me impress this fact on the beginner—if the wing (he refers particularly to the mallard roofing) does not lie parallel with the hook the fly can't swim straight.

It is difficult to keep the cover of the wing on top, but efficiency can only come with practice."

Following the turn of the last century, three gradual changes took place in salmon-fly preference, two of them evolving along parallel directions. We have recently noted the partial revolt against needlessly extravagant fly design that led to the growing popularity of simpler patterns. But many anglers were reluctant to subscribe to this revolt, frequently just giving the trend lip service. That is, they espoused the traditional classics in public while using less ornate flies in private. Generally, however, even the less ornate flies of the period were far from simple by modern standards.

This later trend toward simplicity was very gradual, starting with replacing the ultra-elegant classics with those retaining fishing effectiveness as well as beauty. The trend also winnowed a relatively few designs from the plethora heretofore deemed regionally or generally necessary. No better exposition of this transition exists than that offered by Dr. T. E. Pryce–Tannatt in his *How to Dress Salmon Flies* (1914) discussed in the next chapter. While the good doctor espoused reasonable elegance, he also had a good eye for common sense!

Thus, the turn of the last century saw parallel development in the continuing angling use of the more sensible classics, accompanied by patterns of much greater simplicity as exemplified by those recommended by Chaytor and Crosfield. This trend made the more intricate patterns increasingly scarce because fly dressers found them less profitable as demand for them diminished. Although Kelson and Pryce–Tannatt published nearly four hundred patterns, no more than ten percent of them are currently popular, even with traditionalists.

Since anglers are avid collectors and subject to the law of supply and demand, increasing numbers are seeking old and rare patterns, preferably those exhibiting excellent workmanship and correct ingredients. The third trend, then, in the story of the salmon fly's evolution, sees the transformation of classic patterns from fishing tools to collectible treasures.

CHAPTER TEN

Declination

COLLECTORS who scour the British Isles for classics sometimes locate large turn-of-the-century fly books containing a variety of flies. These usually hold familiar standard patterns rather than many of the more complicated classics that Kelson called "exaggerations." It seems difficult to circumvent the opinion that the latter were intended primarily to demonstrate fly-tying prowess or to serve as conversation pieces, rather than to succeed as fishing lures.

The numerous fly books I have seen in the British Isles usually contain various sizes and duplicates of standard patterns such as *Jock Scott*, the three Doctors, *Silver Grey*, *Mar Lodge*, *Green Highlander*, and *Dusty Miller*, plus others which the former owner fancied and, perhaps, dressings native to the rivers he usually fished. Almost never is there anything more exotic unless it be a few *Pophams*, with their veilings of a dozen or so tiny Indian crow feathers. I can sympathize with this because the beautiful *Popham* is a jewel, but probably no more effective than its poorer relations.

Thus, while the familiar standards are common, other established patterns, indigenous to the countless rivers of the British Isles, add up to hundreds, if not thousands. These plus their infinite variations with their individual histories, components, and dressing techniques, present the opportunity for an absorbing and endless study, a passion that is growing increasingly popular as collectors and fly dressers realize the charms and challenges of this ancient art.

One of the frustrations of this study is acquiring a handsome fly and not knowing what it is. Unidentified flies, like lost children, need roots. Sometimes there is no answer to a fly's identity, but there are always clues. Some will be found herein but, if the pattern was a popular one, we probably would find it in John James Hardy's *Salmon Fishing* (1907). If not, the fly could be a variation of a standard pattern, and perhaps an important one suggesting the work of a renowned expert. Then, too, it might merely be the fabrication of someone's imagination and of only minor interest.

John J. Hardy was a partner in the famous English firm of Hardy Brothers, purveyors of fine flies and tackle for over a century. His book, providing abbreviated patterns for 344 of the most important classic salmon flies, makes it easy to identify an unknown pattern by its characteristics. The pattern names are alphabetically listed down the left column of each of the book's double-page spreads. Heading columns along page tops, in progression of dressings, are listed the components of tag, tail, butt, body, ribbing, hackle, throat, wings, sides, cheeks, horns, and head (when applicable).

Let's presume you have a fly you wish to identify. It has, for example, a black herl butt and a body of orange seal's fur ribbed with silver tinsel. A distinguishing characteristic is the butt, so merely scan down that column of the relatively few patterns with "Blk. hrl" butts until you locate one which also has a body of "O. S fur" (orange seal's fur). The pattern with both of these characteristics is the *Sapper*, a fairly rare one. By checking the fly's other components with those given in the book, the identity can be confirmed. Knowing the pattern is named *Sapper*, you may find more facts about it in other books. These may list minor dressing variations that provide more detailed information.

In Chapter Eight Captain Hale's *How to Tie Salmon Flies* (1892) was discussed, with its dressing of forty patterns. Following the first edition came a second one, published in 1919, and a third in 1930. The latter two contain Hardy's 344 patterns, evidently arranged by Hale with Hardy. In addition Hale added eighteen more patterns: the Scott Series of six classic-type Scottish dressings, and the Gem Series of twelve. The latter features "metallic celluloid" bodies of flies named for, and supposedly remindful of, semiprecious and precious stones. Obviously these were offered strictly for fly-dressing pleasure with little or no thought of their having practical angling use.

So here are three sources of Hardy's original list of classic patterns, fifteen being illustrated on Plate XVII. Since Hardy's and other such books are long out of print, one must locate copies offered by book dealers. The larger dealers frequently advertise in fishing publications and usually offer catalogues for nominal fees deducted from later purchases. One has to shop around to locate titles in the best condition at reasonable prices, but building a library of carefully

HOW TO TIE SALMON FLIES.

A TREATISE ON THE METHODS OF
TYING THE VARIOUS KINDS
OF SALMON FLIES.

WITH   ILLUSTRATED   DIRECTIONS.

BY

MAJOR   J.   H.   HALE

(East Lancashire Regiment).

SECOND EDITION REVISED.
WITH AN APPENDIX GIVING
THE DRESSINGS OF 361 SALMON FLIES,
ALPHABETICALLY ARRANGED.

LONDON:
THE "FISHING GAZETTE," LIMITED,
19, ADAM STREET, STRAND, W.C. 2.
(ALL RIGHTS RESERVED.)
1919.

Title page of Hale's *How to Tie Salmon Flies*, second edition (1919) selected angling books provides constant pleasure, and the books themselves can become a profitable investment.

I like to imagine that the four famous fishing writers who frequented the Three Salmons Hotel in Usk met there together, but it doesn't seem likely. In 1890 Kelson was fifty-four years old, Francis was sixty-eight, and Maxwell was in his early forties; perhaps the first two associated at the famous inn. Pryce–Tannatt, however, was absent, being only nine in 1890. Nevertheless, of the four, he seems the most popular, perhaps because he wrote the most lucidly and held the most practical opinions on angling.

Dr. Thomas Edwin Pryce–Tannatt (1881–1965) was an Englishman who gave up medicine at thirty-one to devote the remainder of his life to angling and its welfare. He not only worked for sporting salmon anglers, but also maintained a balanced overview of their disputes with the salmon-fishing industries in his capacity as Inspector of Salmon Fisheries. He is best known as the author of *How to Dress Salmon Flies* (1914), a book which was republished in a second edition in 1948 and which has since been reprinted.

This sensible and easily understood book on fly-dressing methods, materials, and patterns is considered by many the one volume to own if you can own only one. In nine "lessons," each describing and illustrating the dressing of a specific fly with one of the six types of wings, plus Dee and Spey patterns and grubs, Dr. Pryce–Tannatt lucidly guides his readers through all steps from bare hook to completed product. In the book's appendix he provides detailed and authentic instructions for dressing 100 patterns including examples of the types just mentioned. The book also contains eight full-page illustrations of superb flies photographed in clear and accurate color and reproduced by the then recently (1914) perfected method of four-color-process printing. The color plates in the first edition still are models for publishers to emulate, and I know of none published subsequently considered superior.

Dr. Pryce–Tannatt evidently was a gentleman of the old school. At a time when iron-eyed fly hooks were becoming popular he adhered to those with the old-fashioned gut eyes. If he thought these looked better we can agree with him, but he evidently preferred gut eyes on classic patterns because they were traditional. Some of his favorites are shown on Plates XVIII and XIX.

Note particularly that there are two very different patterns of the beautiful *Evening Star*. One is Pryce–Tannatt's version on Plate XVIII and the other is found in Hale's first edition and illustrated on Plate XXIV. The patterns are given on pages 161 and 162 because they merit being the focal points of any collection.

Pryce–Tannatt's book, in both its color illustrations and its patterns, stresses classics that stood the test of time and were (and are) most commonly used in fishing. It also contains other beautiful examples he evidently couldn't resist, such as his *Evening Star*, a fly more to admire than to use. (I think Hale's dressing is handsomer.) But, with all this, he didn't forget numerous simpler flies that are classics despite their plainness. Since these should be of interest to the novice as well as to the expert, let's select three very attractive ones:

Green Peacock

Tag Silver thread and golden-yellow floss
Tail A topping
Body Pale-blue floss

Ribbing Oval silver tinsel
Throat A pale-blue hackle
Wing Peacock sword feather in strips

Jeannie

Tag Silver tinsel
Tail A topping
Body First third lemon floss, remainder black floss
Ribbing Oval silver tinsel

Throat A (natural) black hackle
Wing Brown mallard strips (set upright)
Sides Jungle cock

Toppy

Tag Silver tinsel
Tail A topping and Indian crow
Butt Claret seal's fur
Body First half, deep-red floss butted with a crimson hackle;

second half, black floss
Ribbing Oval silver tinsel
Throat A black hackle
Wing Bronze white-tipped turkey tail strips (set upright)

These three patterns were usually dressed on rather small hooks (between sizes 4 and 10) and were evidently preferred when rivers ran low.

We see in many of the more recent classic patterns traits reminiscent of ancient flies conceived a century or more ago. Such traits can provide clues to flies' histories or, at least, suggest their provenances. The genealogy of salmon flies could be a book in itself, but the author would have a hard time of it because so much went unrecorded. For inklings, however, note the topping-winged patterns of Plate XVIII (*Black Prince* and *Canary*) and compare them with the *Shannon Goldfinch* and *Golden Butterfly* (Plate V) of the early 1800s. The topping wings provide a clue to the background of these patterns. Or compare the *Stevenson* and *Durham Ranger* (Plate XVIII) with several of the ancient Parsons on Plate V, noting the whole-feather-wing of golden pheasant tippets common to all.

Michael Rogan's method of flaring tippet fibers under a strip-wing roofing was adopted by Ernest Crosfield (page 170) and many other more recent practitioners. Even the *1775 Fly* (page 33) has had many simulations over more than two hundred years; in fact, it is the style basis for a plethora of perennially popular simple patterns. While few will want to bother with such research, these instances link the relatively recent with the remote past.

In retrospect, the Atlantic salmon fly's ancient history evolved from two sources: the inspiration of the "Treatise Twelve" trout patterns of 1496, which had an impact on salmon-fly development for about 250 years; and, secondly, crude flies with such names as *Horse-leech*, *King's Fisher*, and *Libella*, intended for pike but which sometimes hooked salmon. (As we have seen many of the early salmon flies originally were intended to hook pike, an easier fish than salmon to handle on the fly rod. Although intended for pike, however, the flies often drifted into faster flows and hooked salmon—hence the transition.)

The salmon fly's inheritance, or development, then spawned patterns reminiscent of both ancient types, each keeping an identity of its own as shown by such early-nineteenth-century originations as the *Spring Fly* and *Summer Fly* espoused by Bainbridge in 1816 and suitable for salmon even today.

Even before the turn of the nineteenth century two very different schools of thought were independently developing. In England, Scotland, and Wales salmon flies were drab, made from whatever was handy locally on farms or obtained from wildfowling, as exemplified by the patterns of Younger and Scrope in the 1840s. But many decades before that—even prior to 1800—the Irish had brighter ideas! Seafarers and soldiers, returning from far-flung places, brought home colorful bird skins. Finding a market, chiefly in millinery, importations prospered, and Irish fly dressers, eager for new ideas, adopted the brilliant plumage enthusiastically. Such imports were doubtless available around English seaports as well as Irish, but, conditioned to drabness in salmon flies, anglers there evidently disregarded the potential, calling Irish patterns by such epithets as "fish frights."

In spite of such antipathy, the beauty of the Irish patterns was appealing, and a period of coexistence developed around midcentury with the gaudier Irish imports enjoying increasing popularity. The extent of this brilliance varied widely, depending on the solidity of established opinion and the local availablility of colorful materials. Even where the gaudy didn't predominate, however, it did influence the drab, resulting in a third new type of salmon fly, a sort of hybrid. Examples of these are found on Plates VI and VII.

Soon after the turn of this century, conservative heads, more attuned to practicability than pretension, termed the brilliant excesses "elaborate nonsense," and angling patterns developed in two parallel directions. One was toward simplicity and concentrated on essentials without fripperies. The other winnowed down the gaudier classics to a few dozen practical patterns, including some standard favorites that still remain popular.

More recently a third trend has emerged in which angling is minimized in favor of collectible art. While this faction considers collectible every fly of historic value, it specializes in the most meticulously made examples of complicated classic salmon-fly dressing, usually reproduced by dedicated contemporaries who study and emulate old methods, using the best authentic materials obtainable. This burgeoning group of artisans and collectors is the subject of our final chapter.

Before turning to salmon flies as collectors' items, however, we discuss the use of the classic patterns, and others, in the United States and Canada. And, turning to North America, we find the thought still persists: following their experiments with mohair and dog's hair wings, why didn't dressers in the United Kingdom establish the American-style hair-winged salmon fly, the essence of practical simplicity? If they once thought it too plebeian, they surely don't now.

North America enjoys the beautifully feathered classics as much as the British do, but perhaps for another reason. They had a profound influence on the development of the American salmon fly; an innovation that has reverberated all around the Atlantic. So now, let's turn to our side of the pond to see how it all came about!

CHAPTER ELEVEN

Americanization

BEFORE the dawning of the nineteenth century Atlantic salmon were prolific in most rivers from Canada to as far south as Connecticut. There, as one account relates, wagon drivers wouldn't ford streams in season because the horses frightened the thickly packed salmon, and their rushings and splashings made the teams bolt. The fish were so thick, and so easily speared or netted, that there was no need to fish for them with hook and line.

In the late 1700s and early 1800s, however, salmon in the northeastern United States began to decline and in some streams became nonexistent. Industries had dammed the rivers, preventing the fish from reaching their spawning grounds. Overnetting of the declining stocks, plus pollution from mill refuse and sewage, did the rest. On the Connecticut River, for example, there were plenty of salmon until 1798, when a high dam was built below the mouth of the Miller's River tributary. Salmon were caught below the dam for a decade or two afterward, but by 1820 their elimination was complete. Similar disaster befell the Merrimac River about 1870. Previously Daniel Webster (1782–1852) is quoted in *Wildwood's Magazine* (1888) as having said that he "remembered the time when the Merrimac was crowded with salmon, but nobody thought of taking them with a hook." We can't help but ponder the rapid destruction of this priceless resource and the apparent lack of any effort to prevent it.

The declining salmon stocks stimulated interest in fishing for salmon with rod and line. Accounts of fly-fishing were rare until the last quarter of the nineteenth century partly because anglers lacked the knowhow but also because would-be salmon fishers had to undergo tedious travel to the Maine rivers where salmon still existed, or as far as the wildernesses of Canada, where salmon stocks remained relatively untouched.

Sport fishing for salmon made headway, however. An interesting account appeared in the August 12, 1880, issue of *Forest and Stream* which said in part: "In proof that they [the salmon] now take the manufactured insect we publish the following dispatch which was received at Portland from Bangor one day last week: 'J. F. Leavitt and H. L. Leonard—the rod man—have just returned from a trip and have brought with them the first salmon taken with a fly on Penobscott waters.'"

The account doesn't say what the successful fly was. Of course, Hiram Leonard then was in the split-bamboo rod-making business in a small brick building on the Bangor hillside, in company with Fred E. Thomas and William L. Edwards. Nearby, on the Penobscot, is the famous Bangor salmon pool, which provided a declining salmon fishery until 1938. Although Leonard and Edwards left the partnership about 1880, the work was carried on by Fred Thomas, followed, for a time, by his son, Leon.

This grim account of the American salmon's decline has a happy sequel. As this is being written (in 1986) the New England states have joined with conservation organizations to restore the Atlantic salmon fishery in the Connecticut, Merrimac, Penobscot, and other important rivers and their many branches. While there is not yet rod fishing in the Connecticut and Merrimac, over 300 salmon returned to the former in 1985 and over 200 to the latter. The Penobscot now allows fly-fishing, and at least 3,000 salmon were counted as having returned to it in 1986, of which over 625 were taken on fly.

Perhaps the greatest angling thrill this author ever had was to land a bright nine-pound hen fish in June 1985 in a pool just above the breached Bangor dam. Finally, a salmon caught in home territory! Many dedicated people have joined this sometimes frustrating restoration project, but it seems to be growing more successful year after year. While we enjoy the results of the restorers' efforts, let us raise our glasses in grateful toasts to all who have worked so hard to make domestic sport fishing for Atlantic salmon possible.

With the dearth of turn-of-the-century salmon fishing in the North Atlantic states, and the growing interest in it, anglers turned to Canada for their sport.

Early ones usually had to camp out. It was a relaxing journey by luxurious steam train to a town or city nearest the river one desired to fish, such as Campbellton and Bathurst in New Brunswick, or Matapedia in Quebec. There, an outfitter would provide food and equipment and suggest guides and a cook. These were French–Canadians, Indians, or mixed bloods who were expert with their birch-bark canoes and steel-shod fir pike poles. Their salary was about a dollar a day, perhaps a bit less for the cook.

With canoes loaded, the guides would click their poles into the gravel and speedily push their crafts upstream to a predetermined camping spot, perhaps with time to fish along the way. At the destination the guides erected wall-tents for their sports and fixed bough beds for them to sleep on. The guides spent the nights curled up in blankets near the fire or under canoes when it rained. Several days might be spent at one place if the fishing was good. Provisions were re-plenished at remote farms along the river. On such trips in the early days wealthy anglers might find a favorite point of land near good salmon pools and be able to buy it. They then would erect a log lodge with a wide porch around it, and small outbuildings for guides and equipment. Some of these lodges were large and palatial, providing luxurious summer homes for owners and guests all through the fishing seasons.

An unusual mode of transportation allowed anglers to travel in what was called a "horse-yacht." It was a houseboat towed by from two to four—usually three—horses, and it would more appropriately have been called a scow (although that was considered rather vulgar). This conveyance was a sturdy rectangular flat-bottomed boat which drew about eight inches of water. It was about 50 feet long and 10 feet wide. There was a forward deck about 15 feet long behind which was a peak-roofed house, or cabin, or cottage, with cots and open space for a dining table, a stove, and some chairs. Aft of the wall of this little room was a shelved pantry and a chest for provisions. This opened into a kitchen and a sleeping room for the boatmen. About eight such conveyances operated on the Restigouche around the end of the nineteenth century. The idea was derived from the big, low-draft scows used for hauling lumbering equipment up-river. All that was needed was a little house.

The horse-yacht was steered by a large rudder controlled by a long tiller which could be operated from the roof of the boat by the helmsman. The horses usually were harnessed abreast and hitched to the yacht by a long rope. When all was loaded and ready, the driver, who rode the middle horse, would urge the team into the river; the yacht would scrape over the gravel until it floated and,

A HORSE-YACHT

A favorite means of transportation and base of operations on the Ristigouche around the
turn of the last century. (Drawing by Charles DeFeo)

with the anglers sitting comfortably on the foredeck, the contrivance would be
pulled upstream at a speed of about three miles an hour, with canoes in tow.

Horse-yachts were used mainly on the Restigouche, a wide river with rapids
but without waterfalls. Near nightfall the craft was tied to shore, and sports and
guides took to canoes for evening fishing. Stops were made along the way at
farms for provisions or at lodges for sociability. Such river trips could take a
month or more. There was no hurry then and everyone was ready to enjoy the
wilderness solitude and the superb angling for huge salmon and smaller sea trout.

When the time came for returning, the horses were put on deck for the drift downstream; a reward they must have enjoyed after their labors.

Although the salmon flies used in Canada around the turn of the century were largely the more popular British classic patterns, others were exclusively North American. Thaddeus Norris describes some of them in his *American Angler's Book* (1864), "by far the most important American work on fishing." Uncle Thad, as he liked to be called, was a Virginian who was born in 1811 and who lived in Philadelphia until his death in 1877. His book is a general one with a chapter dealing with salmon flies. He says:

> Very few of the flies imported from England and Ireland are suitable for the rivers of New Brunswick, being generally too large and showy for those clear waters. The gaudy Irish flies tied for the Shannon would frighten the salmon on this side of the Atlantic, while others would not be noticed by them. The profuse variety of beautiful but useless flies imposed on some of our verdant countrymen, with full pockets, by London and Dublin tackle-makers, is astonishing. An accomplished salmon fisher of St. John, with whom I had the pleasure of fishing for two weeks last summer, had only two standard flies for the Miramichi and Nipisiguit; one the *Blue and Brown* the other the *Silver Grey*, the latter for high water. The Blue and Brown, by tying with darker tinted hackles and bodies, as the water clears, he uses almost entirely. This has become so famous amongst the anglers of the province that it has taken his name, the *Nicholson* fly [shown on Plate XX].

This is the pattern:

—————————————————————— *Nicholson* ——————————————————————

Tag Flat gold tinsel	from end of body, also forming the throat
Tail Mallard, and a few fibers of golden pheasant breast feather	*Wing* Brown mallard strips, sparse
Body Blood-red seal's fur	*Collar* Black ostrich herl
Ribbing Oval gold tinsel	*Head* Black
Hackle A blue and a blood-red hackle	

Uncle Thad says about this fly: "The dubbing and hackle of this fly should be of deeper tint as the water becomes clearer. The angler whose name it bears gives the tail and wings an upright set, giving it a peculiarly gay appearance."

Norris recommends dark, sober tints except when waters are high and/or discolored. Then he prefers lighter ones, including pale yellow, pearl, and light grey. He is especially fond of patterns eleven and twelve in *The Book of the Salmon* by Edward Fitzgibbon (Ephemera) (1847) as shown on Plate VII. He adds, "In addition to the flies I have described there are several tied by John Chamberlain that are of great repute on the Nipisiguit. Among them is one I will describe." (See Plate XX). Norris's dressing is as follows:

Chamberlain

Tag	Fine oval gold tinsel			black floss and continued for the throat
Body	One fourth bright-yellow floss; remainder, black floss		*Wing*	Strips of brown mallard or wild turkey
Ribbing	Oval gold tinsel, from tag		*Collar*	Black ostrich (optional)
Hackle	A blood-red hackle over the		*Head*	Black

Norris says, "Dr. Adamson, in *Salmon Fishing in Canada* (1860) gives the following list of flies used on the rivers emptying into the St. Lawrence: *Louise, Edwin, Forsyth, Stephens, Ross, Parson, Strachan* and *Langevin*." Most of these are illustrated on Plate XX, and it will be noted that not all are quite as "sober" as Uncle Thad recommended!

A doughty Scottish artillery officer named Captain Campbell Hardy roamed Nova Scotia and the Restigouche region in the 1860s and wrote about canoe camping and fishing there in his *Forest Life in Acadie* (1869). He says: "The flies for the Nipisiguit should be small and neat, and of three sizes for each pattern for different states of water. . . . Small grey-bodied flies ribbed with silver, grey legs, and wing mixed with wood duck and golden pheasant will do well. Many other and brighter flies may be used in the rough water."

Evidently Captain Hardy would favor several of the patterns shown on Plate XX. I have long held the theory that a bright, a medium, and a dark fly, each in several sizes, should be basics in every salmon angler's kit, and the captain seems to agree.

In 1884 Robert Barnwell Roosevelt (Theodore Roosevelt's uncle) added to American angling literature his *The Game Fish of the North*, a general angling book containing nothing new about tackle, tactics, and information about Atlantic salmon with the exception of eight fly dressings. He gives the patterns for the ten salmon flies printed in Thaddeus Norris's book and provides proper credit to Dr. Adamson. The new eight are the *Captain, Cariboo, Darling, Emmet, Grey Fly, Lillie, Major,* and *Whitcher*. While attractive to fly dressers and worthy of historic interest, all but one have fallen into obscurity. (The *Captain* and *Major*, and the *Louise* mentioned by Norris, are of British origin.) That one fly is the *Grey Fly*.

———————————————— *Grey Fly* ————————————————

Tag Silver wire and deep-orange floss

Tail A small topping and sprigs of grey mallard

Body Grey mohair

Ribbing Fine oval silver tinsel

Hackle Grey, with carmine at throat

Wing Mixed, of mallard, turkey, tippet, topping, and blue macaw

Head Black, with black ostrich herl

The *Grey Fly* is a cousin of the *Nipisiguit Grey*, which, except for the body, is similar to the famous British *Silver Grey*. The "Nip" is a popular North American pattern midway between a dark and a bright one, and is dressed as follows:

———————————————— *Nipisiguit Grey* ————————————————

Tag Fine oval silver tinsel and bright-yellow floss

Tail A small topping

Butt Two or three turns of peacock herl or black wool

Body Medium-grey wool, not built up

Ribbing Fine oval silver tinsel

Throat A few turns of a grizzly hackle, tied as a collar and pulled down

Wing In four sections, two on each side, of bronze mallard

Head Black

Modern anglers simplify these two patterns and often prefer a grey hair-wing, such as squirrel tail or grey fox. Many use a silver body, as in the *Silver Grey.*

One of the anglers who canoed up the Restigouche before 1876 was Dean Sage (1841–1902), a New York lumber baron who wrote *The Ristigouche and Its Salmon Fishing* in 1888. This rare and expensive book was reprinted in 1973 by The Anglers and Shooters Press, which also reprinted the second edition of George M. Kelson's *The Salmon Fly* in 1979. Both books were beautifully reproduced and are very faithful to the originals.

Mr. Sage's favorite part of the Restigouche was thirty miles upriver where it is joined by its tributary, the Upsalquitch. He and his party camped there for several years, and he later acquired a large river frontage and built a crude lodge. Considering this too primitive, he later constructed a much larger and very palatial log structure which he named Camp Harmony, with broad porches looking out over both rivers, a tremendous octagonal peaked-roof dining-living room, and two wings for sleeping quarters.

This pretentious building was designed by Stanford White, the famous architect, who was a frequent visitor. Mr. White is remembered for two things in particular. He was the originator of the aptly named *Night Hawk* salmon fly, still a great favorite, and he was shot to death in 1906 by an irate Harry K. Thaw when the latter found him having dinner with Thaw's wife, the showgirl Evelyn Nesbit. Fortunately, these two events occurred in an order favorable to anglers. This is the dressing, as illustrated on Plate XX, for White's fly:

Night Hawk

Tag Oval silver tinsel and yellow floss

Tail A short topping, over which are one or two fibers of blue kingfisher, half as long as the topping

Butt Two or three turns of red wool

Body Flat silver tinsel

Ribbing Oval silver tinsel

Wing Two sections of a black feather extending to the tip of the tail, and a topping

Throat A small bunch of black hackle fibers, rather short

Shoulders Jungle cock, half as long as the wing

Cheeks Sections of a blue kingfisher feather, set outside and over the jungle cock, nearly as long as it but narrow enough to not conceal it

Head Red

The hair-wing version is as above except there is no floss in the tag, no cheeks, and no topping. The jungle cock is short, and the wing is of black hair.

Mr. Sage's sumptuous book is filled with fascinating accounts of the luxurious side of salmon fishing before the turn of the century. He relates experiences concerning salmon-fly selection. Here are some examples:

> There is a beautiful and good pool at the foot of the Chain of Rocks. It gives good fishing and Mr. John Wilmot killed there in one afternoon ten salmon, the smallest above 20 pounds and the largest 42 pounds. These were all taken with one fly tied for the occasion by the angler.

Dean Sage doesn't give the dressing, but I have taken it from the color plate of favorite flies from his book, and it is reproduced on Plate XX.

--- *Wilmot* ---

Tag   Short silver tinsel

Tail   A very short topping

Butt   Red ostrich or similar (see body)

Body   Black and red, mixed, with just enough red to show, probably of seal's fur. The butt may have been of same material. The body is rough, like a caterpillar's, and is of same diameter throughout, same as butt

Ribbing   Fine oval silver tinsel, or twist

Throat   Probably black and brown grouse, or similar, as a collar, quite short, same length as gape of hook

Wing   Four fairly narrow strips of married wing sections extending to end of tail. Each is two thirds black-and-brown-mottled turkey or similar, married to one third white goose underneath. Each section is separate and pointed

Head   Black, with gut eye

Mr. Sage's account of Canadian salmon water and fishing continues:

Many flies resemble certain insects and look altogether differently when wet and in the water from what they do when dry. The *Jock Scott*, for instance (an excellent fly on the Ristigouche) when dry has a very gaudy appearance; wet it, and it will be seen to have quite a different and sober effect.

The *Durham Ranger* resembles very strongly the black and red butterfly which is frequent in Canadian rivers, and other killing flies are like certain

Title page of Sage's *The Ristigouche and Its Salmon Fishing* (1888)

known insects. The wingless flies, with heavy hackles, resembling caterpillars and grubs, have been successfully used to take salmon.

Most people agree that for early fishing the flies should be large (but) I have found that of those which are very bright, such as the *Durham Ranger*, quite a small one is advisable. I should say that the best results in the early fishing follow the use of good-sized sober flies, and would put at the head of these the *Jock Scott* which, though bright-looking when dry, has quite the contrary effect in the water.

As the hours of sunshine lengthen the fish become more dainty in their feeding and only occasionally feel the disposition towards the large, fat, and sometimes gaudy insects which they craved a short time before. . . . I can almost say that for the late low-water fishing no fly can be too small.

Another of the greatest and most historic of Canadian salmon rivers is the Grand Cascapedia, which flows southward near the middle of the Gaspé Peninsula into the Bay of Chaleurs. This is the home river of another great American pattern in the classic style, the famous *Lady Amherst*, for so many years the favorite on this big river.

The *Lady Amherst* was originated about 1925 by George D. B. Bonbright, president of the Seaboard Airline Railway. Charles Phair, author of *Atlantic Salmon Fishing* (1937) says he commercialized the pattern under the name of *Bonbright No. 2* to distinguish it from Mr. Bonbright's earlier streamer fly of that name, which is a salt-water pattern designed for tarpon. The change of name to *Lady Amherst* was to avoid confusion and feature the Amherst pheasant feathers dominating the wing. Guides on the Grand Cascapedia around the middle of the century thought so much of it that it often was the only pattern they wanted their sports to use, normally in sizes as large as 5/0 for that big river. The *Lady Amherst* is a true American classic. This is the proper dressing, as shown on Plate XX:

─────────────── *Lady Amherst* ───────────────

Tag Fine oval silver tinsel and golden-yellow floss

Tail A topping and strands of teal

Butt Black ostrich

Body Flat silver tinsel

Ribbing Oval silver tinsel

Hackle Badger, from butt, sparse

Wing Two jungle cock feathers back to back extending to end of tail, veiled with two square-ended Amherst pheasant tippets, one on each side, the inner bars of which lie over the butt. Over these on each side is a shorter round-ended Amherst pheasant tippet extending to the inner bars of the longer tippets so the outer black bars of the shorter feathers cover the inner black bars of the longer feathers (as in Ranger patterns)

Sides Jungle cock

Cheeks Blue chatterer (or kingfisher)

Topping A golden pheasant crest feather

Horns Blue and yellow macaw

Head Black

A few of the British classics always have been popular on Canadian rivers, including the *Jock Scott, Silver Grey, Dusty Miller, Thunder & Lightning, Mar Lodge,* and the simpler *Silver Blue* and *Blue Charm.* The *Black Dose* has been Americanized in various ways, including by giving it a mostly black hair-wing. As usual everywhere, each North American river has its favorites, patterns that anglers through experience have come to have faith in. For example, during the first half of this century about fifty percent of the salmon taken on the Grand Cascapedia fell to the *Lady Amherst,* a fly which, paradoxically, seemed to be of minor importance everywhere else.

Only two patterns can be called tried-and-true American classics in the British sense: the *Lady Amherst* and the *Night Hawk.* Several of the others mentioned might have earned this distinction had not angling whims forced them into obscurity. Nevertheless they are attractive patterns of historic interest and certainly worthy of attention by collectors.

Why so few North American classics? I can think of three reasons. First, we seem to prefer practical simplicity over complicated tradition, adhering mostly to the doctrines of Crosfield and Chaytor. Secondly, we are more inclined to use the dry fly when conditions are suitable, thereby enjoying the thrills for surface strikes. Finally, simple hair-wing patterns attained their success and popularity here, confirming the victory of pulsating hair over less mobile feathers.

The decline of the classics became apparent about 1930 when Jack Russell, proprietor of a famous fishing camp on the Miramichi and author of *Jill and I and the Salmon* (1950) complacently said, "There has been little change in the basic [classic] patterns of flies from the beginning of salmon angling on this continent. The standard [classic] patterns hold good year after year."

Perhaps Jack was unaware that pioneers in hair-wing development were very busy in the 1930s and 1940s. From records of the International Game Fish Association, which maintains statistics on the fly patterns used in catching record salmon, it is plain that classics did rule until about 1950, but then hair-wings such as *Rusty Rat* and *Silver Rat* began to make inroads.

Let's not protest that hair-wings don't belong in a book about classic patterns. Many hair-wings have their roots in the classic older flies. To bring this account up to date we must consider them, although we lack the benefit of foresight to determine how they will be evaluated by future anglers.

CHAPTER TWELVE

Modernization

$\mathcal{L}$ONGER AGO than I care to admit (but about 1930 on the Matapedia River) I shared a pool with a gentleman I'll never forget. He was old. I wasn't. He was a club member. I was only a guest. He selected a favorite spot, and I took care to give him plenty of room. Near noon I noticed him sitting beside the pool fussing with his tackle, so I approached him respectfully.

He greeted me cheerfully, while withdrawing from his kit a magnificent leather fly book containing an awe-inspiring collection of beautiful classics, from which he selected a *Jock Scott* I immediately coveted. Plucking a pin from his lapel, to my horror he began to scrape it through the wing to separate its fibers; persisting until this was done thoroughly.

"It seems a shame to treat a beautiful fly that way," I ventured. "Why don't you use a hair-wing of similar pattern?"

The old angler shook his head. "I've always used traditional patterns," he said, "and I guess I'll never change. Trouble with them is, they don't have enough action, so I separate all the fibers to make the wing pulsate in the water. I hook more salmon that way."

This is perhaps the main reason why the classic feather-wing type of dressing declined in favor of the modern and popular hair-wing. The hair-wing is often considered a North American development, but we have seen that it was used in the British Isles late in the past century, and perhaps not so very late at that.

Tradition-bent but practical American anglers, rather than giving up the classics entirely, modernized some of them to hair-wing versions. *Thunder & Lightning, Green Highlander, Jock Scott, Blue Doctor*, and *Black Dose*, shown on Plate XXI, are good examples. Modification merely consists of generally following the classic dressing, eliminating nonessentials as desired, and substituting hair for feathers in the wing. The coloration of the hair roughly follows that of the classic pattern, usually applied more sparsely for deeper fishing. I have had excellent success with Doctor patterns dressed this way, but my favorite is the hair-winged *Black Dose*, as follows:

Black Dose

Tag Silver tinsel and yellow floss

Tail A topping and very few red hackle fibers

Body Black floss or wool

Ribbing Fine oval silver tinsel

Hackle A black hackle up body, with two or three turns for throat

Wing Black bear hair mixed with three or four peacock sword fibers

Cheeks Jungle cock

Head Black

The hotbed of American modernization seems to be during the 1930s and 1940s on the Miramichi River, New Brunswick, in the region of Doaktown, where pioneers such as Everett Price, Bert Miner, Fred Merseau, Sandy Munn, Everett Lyons, Van Storey, Ira Gruber, and others were experimenting with simplified feather- and hair-winged patterns and were catching more fish with them than with traditional British classics.

Ira Gruber, as related in my *Atlantic Salmon Flies & Fishing* (1970) was a Pennsylvania cotton mill owner who retired to his beloved Miramichi River in 1915 to spend the rest of his life hunting and fishing. He was famous for twenty named patterns of which sixteen were simple feather-wings and four were hair-wings. At a time when people thought salmon too difficult to catch when the water ran low and clear, Mr. Gruber proved it could be done with simple patterns as small as 10s and 12s.

In this, unbeknownst to him, Gruber was the American counterpart of A. H. E. Wood, of Cairnton, on the River Dee, the British exponent of the sparse low-water fly on the floating line, who was conducting similar experiments at about the same time. Wood had access to light-wire, low-water hooks, and evidently Gruber didn't, but their successes were similar. (Wood's will be outlined later in this chapter.)

While Gruber's flies were prominent for a time and influenced modernization, I have noticed only one popular on the Miramichi recently. This is the pretty and simple *Oriole*.

──────────────────────── *Oriole* ────────────────────────

Tail	A few fibers from a brown-red body feather of golden pheasant			pulled downward and extending nearly to point of hook
Body	Black wool, cigar shaped		*Wing*	Several fibers from a brown-red body feather of golden pheasant roofed with doubled grey mallard dyed pale green
Ribbing	Fine oval silver tinsel, with two turns taken under the tail, as a tag			
Throat	A brown hackle, as a collar,		*Head*	Black

Like their earlier upriver counterparts in the British Isles, these anglers and fly tiers usually lacked access to fancy ingredients. They made do with what they had, and prominent in their kits was the fur of black bear, squirrel, and wood-chuck.

One of the earliest American patterns, dated 1920 or before, was an all-black one aptly named the *Black Bear* and said to have been originated by Harry Smith of Cherryfield, Maine. Although crude and simple, it proved that fancy, exotic patterns weren't necessary for hooking salmon. The pattern still is one of the best, modernized with a floss butt (now usually fluorescent) of any color but ordinarily green, red, or yellow, and so identified in the fly's name. An example is shown on Plate XXI.

──────────────── *Black Bear (Green Butt)* ────────────────

Tag	Two or three turns of silver wire or fine oval silver tinsel		*Ribbing*	Silver wire or fine oval silver tinsel
Butt	Lime-green fluorescent floss, fairly wide		*Throat*	Two or three turns of a lime-green hackle, as a collar
Tail	A short section of above, like a veiling		*Wing*	A small bunch of black bear hair extending to end of tail
Body	Black floss		*Head*	Black

While the *Lady Amherst* was paramount on the Grand Cascapedia, the less glamorous *Red Abbey* was a pet of the Restigouche. It has been a favorite pattern there since 1913 and still is a good producer in all sizes, often dressed on double hooks. This is the dressing, as illustrated on Plate XXI.

Red Abbey

Tag	Flat embossed or oval silver tinsel
Tail	A small section of fibers of a red feather
Body	Red floss
Ribbing	Flat embossed or oval silver tinsel

Throat	A few turns of a brown hackle applied as a collar, pulled down and tied back slightly
Wing	A small bunch of light-brown squirrel tail or brown bucktail
Cheeks	Jungle cock (optional)
Head	Black or red

The *Silver Abbey* is a favorite fish producer. It is the same except that the body is of flat silver tinsel.

Another famous and currently still popular pattern is the *Cosseboom*, originated about 1923 on the Margaree River, Nova Scotia, by John C. Cosseboom, poet, newspaper writer, champion fly-caster, and peripatetic salmon angler, who lived in Woonsocket, Rhode Island, between 1885 and 1935. I knew John only through friends who fished with him, but they told me the *Cosseboom* was intended to imitate a greenish caterpillar, a simulation the *Wooly Worm* variation should effect as well.

In any event, the *Cosseboom* suffered from the popular trend of changing the original dressing into numerous variations of different colors, none of which match the original in effectiveness. The popular original (often dressed incorrectly) is as follows:

Cosseboom

Tag	Embossed silver tinsel
Tail	Olive-green floss, cut off short
Body	Olive-green floss, moderately slim (Pearsall's shade No. 82)
Ribbing	Embossed silver tinsel

Wing	A small bunch of grey squirrel tail hairs extending to the end of the tail
Hackle	A lemon-yellow hackle tied on as a collar after the wing is

applied and slanting backward
to merge with the top of the
wing

Cheeks Jungle cock (optional)
Head Red

This fly often is dressed as a bucktail—that is, it is made on a longer hook to imitate a bait fish. As such it is popular for trout and other species. The value of bucktails or streamers should not be underestimated as experimental weapons when salmon fishing becomes frustrating. They often succeed as a change of pace when fished by various methods. In such cases one pattern seems about as good as another but, especially in Maine, the *Herb Johnson Special*, for unknown reasons, seems extremely effective. This may be due to its relative brightness. Bright flies do well in high or discolored water. The simple and even brighter *Mickey Finn* is another popular example.

When periods of low and clear water make fishing difficult, small flies, such as Ira Gruber advocated, often can solve the problem when used on light leaders. As mentioned earlier, Gruber's counterpart in Scotland was Arthur H. E. Wood, who leased about two miles of the Aberdeenshire Dee at Cairnton, a bit upriver from the quaint town of Banchory. It was here the famous Bessie Brown dressed her beautiful salmon flies and taught the art of bagpipe playing, excelling equally in both arts.

While Mr. Gruber's solution for hooking frustrating fish was to use very small flies, Mr. Wood preferred a system he originated featuring sparsely dressed low-water patterns—that is, flies tied on long-shanked light-wire hooks a size or two larger than normal for the dressing applied. Thus the dressing usually extends no farther than to above the hook's point. Examples of such patterns are illustrated on Plate XXII. Their purpose is to afford superior hooking ability.

The system Mr. Wood advocated was called the "Greased Line Method" (modernly, using the "floating line") where the cast was made across or slightly upstream with enough slack at the end to allow the fly to drift freely sideways very near the surface. To accomplish this correctly, experience in completely mending the line is necessary. Much greater detail can be found in *Greased Line Fishing for Salmon* (1937) by "Jock Scott" (Donald Rudd), who quotes Mr. Wood:

> I like the dressing to be as thin, transparent and misty as possible where the low water flies are concerned. The older and thinner a fly becomes through wear, the better the fish seem to like it, providing the weather is hot and the

water clear. I have caught fish on a practically bare hook on which there was left no body and only the head and four fibers of the wings; also quite a number on a hook with only the body and no wing or hackle at all.

As regards pattern, I do not believe that this matters at all. *Blue Charm* and *Silver Blue* are my stock, simply on the principle that one is more or less black and the other white and so give *me* a choice. I once fished through the whole season with a *March Brown* only, and got my share, and more, of the fish caught.

I always start with a *Blue Charm* and only change it if all the sizes I try prove no good, then I try a *Silver Blue*. But if the water is very clear and the weather bright, I use a *March Brown*, and pick out the "ripest" one in my box.

If you have the right size fly on it is very rarely that you get merely a rise; the fish always means business if he comes. If, however, he rises and refuses, it is a clear sign that the fly is too big and too showy for him.

Such cogent comments by Mr. Wood indicate the value of Mr. Rudd's book. Mr. Wood's affinity for the *March Brown* was, at least in part, due to the prevalence, in season on the river, of the insect which it simulated. My experience with Mr. Wood's method is limited because, under conditions where it is advisable, I prefer the dry fly. In support of it, however, from 1913 to 1934 (the year of Mr. Wood's death) he landed a total of 3,540 salmon, most caught, presumably, by using his method.

I do remember one week on Iceland's Langá when I fished with a Puerto Rican gentleman who was a devoted disciple of Mr. Wood. I noted his enviable success with the greased-line method, even to hooking a salmon or two on a bare hook whose shank was painted red, which was the culmination of Mr. Wood's theory of near-surface drifting of sparse and small dressings! (Examples of normal Dee patterns for average and high water are illustrated on Plate X.)

Mr. Wood's success with frazzled flies "with only the body and no wing or hackle at all" seems to provide a rationale for using nymphs in salmon fishing. These might be useful during summer conditions, perhaps by usual methods, but especially by using Mr. Wood's. Examples of salmon nymphs by Ted Niemeyer and Charles De Feo are included on the lower half of Plate XXII.

One of the inconsistencies of salmon-fly design and selection is that nearly every river (and even sections of the river) has a set of flies indigenous to it that the anglers there feel will hook salmon to the exclusion of most others. These regional patterns exceed by far the generally accepted ones supposedly good everywhere. A theory is advanced that the salmon indigenous to each river make up an exclusive ethnic group with habits conditioned by nature varying from those of other fish in other rivers. This theory maintains that the salmon of each river have discrete characteristics influencing their reactions to the colors, and types of flies and even to their methods of presentation. In other words, find the keys to the salmons' proclivities on an individual river, and you will have more success there (but not necessarily anywhere else).

This might account for the variations in flies and angling methods we observe to be popular on the rivers discussed herein. It indicates that the advice of experienced guides may be more valuable than it is often considered to be. It suggests that if we don't know the answers, it is advantageous to experiment until we discover patterns and presentations that give best results on any individual river.

There may be no better recent example of this than on the Penobscot in Maine, where the salmon run has been restored in recent years to the extent that restricted fly-fishing is now permitted. Let's pay it a short visit, because it portends what we hope will soon happen on other New England rivers.

On this cotton-cloudy but bright June morning we follow a wooded path to the river, ending at a secluded spot a half-mile or so below the Veasie Dam slightly upstream from Bangor. A dozen or so anglers perch on logs under big trees gossiping and watching the action. This is provided by about an equal number of anglers slowly wading near shore along the wide and deep river as they cast quartering downstream in safely separated procession. The leader steps ashore on reaching the end of fishable water, while another man wades out to join the end of the single line. Thus, each man takes his turn in line as it comes up, spending as much time sitting as fishing.

The sitting is educational and interesting. Flies are compared, ideas exchanged, food nibbled, news and jokes related. Suddenly one of the rods hooks a salmon. Anglers near the action reel in and come ashore. One of the men picks up a large net and stands near the fortunate angler, whose active fish may take him around a bend downstream.

The angler brings the fish to net as quickly as prudence permits to avoid exhausting it. Grasping it nearest the tail, he frees it from hook and net, holding it up momentarily before returning it to the water. There he moves it back and forth against the current until it revives and swims away. About half of landed salmon are released; the others kept, abiding by strict rationing regulations.

No need for wardens here! Each angler acts as one, quick to spot and correct abuses, which, indeed, are rare. These sportsmen have fought bureaucracy and aided conservation for many years to make this restoration possible. Each belongs to one or more local clubs whose purposes are partly social but mainly to foster the abundant return of Atlantic salmon, a species they regard less as quarry and more as respected guests they have been responsible for inviting.

Across the wide river a similar group is in action, this one less processional, with anglers variously located. Other groups are out of sight elsewhere. Small boats are anchored or cruising for better locations, with one or two anglers in each. Despite all this, the river seems far from crowded. Visiting anglers are welcome, but they are advised that the size of the river makes it wise to seek an experienced guide.

Despite the recent reclamation, anglers on the Penobscot have already developed two important patterns that will be given here, and have adapted a few others for their use. Depending on the volume of the river, these often are used in large sizes, even as big as 5/0.

Prominent among the purely Penobscot originations are the *Wringer* and *Coburn Special*:

Wringer

Tag	Flat silver tinsel and golden-yellow floss	*Throat*	Medium-blue hackle fibers
Tail	A topping	*Wing*	Grey squirrel tail hair dyed red under same dyed yellow, in equal amounts
Butt	Black ostrich herl		
Body	Black floss	*Head*	Black
Ribbing	Fine oval silver tinsel		

Coburn Special

Tag	Two or three turns of fine oval silver tinsel	*Wing*	A small bunch of grey squirrel tail hairs dyed green, over which is an equal amount of the same dyed red
Tail	A small bunch of grey squirrel tail hairs dyed green		
Body	Light-green fluorescent floss, built up, with a midbutt of black ostrich herl	*Hackle*	Yellow, as a collar, sparse and tied back
		Head	Black

This pattern also is made in two other color combinations: red body, red under black squirrel tail wing, matching tail, and black hackle. Also, yellow body, orange under black squirrel tail wing, matching tail, and black hackle. The midbutt is the same on all three versions.

The *Black Bear* (see page 195) is varied by a green over black hair tail, and a wing of grey squirrel dyed lime green over which are a few peacock sword fibers. This is then called the *C. Z. Special.* The *Black Bear* with a red butt is varied by a red- over black-hair tail, a black bear hair wing over a bit of red hair topped with a few peacock sword fibers, and a bright-red fairly long hackle collar. This pattern is called *Foxfire.*

While the above patterns originated on the Penobscot, they merit swims anywhere, including other Maine rivers which permit fly-fishing: the Narraguagus, Denny's, Machias, Pleasant, and Sheepscot. Dan Gapen's ever useful *Muddler Minnow* is successful on these rivers too, but even more so when made all orange, preferably with fine gold tinsel ribbing. It then becomes a substitute for the famous *General Practitioner.*

Primarily dressed as a bucktail, but also tied salmon-style, the *Herb Johnson Special* was originated about 1960 by Herbert Johnson of Yarmouth, Maine. Either way, it is amazingly effective and strongly recommended. This is the correct dressing:

—————————— *Herb Johnson Special* ——————————

Body Black wool, fairly full

Ribbing Embossed flat silver tinsel (wound in reverse, toward tier)

Throat White bucktail, as long as the wing

Wing A very small bunch of bright-yellow bucktail, slightly longer than the hook; on each side of this two strands each of red and blue fluorescent nylon floss; and on each side above the floss one strand of peacock herl; over this a rather sparse bunch of brown bucktail dyed yellow. (All components are of the same length, slightly longer than the hook)

Head Silver paint, with a yellow eye and black pupil

We might ask why streamers or bucktails, and similar low-winged, large-size salmon flies, are so often effective for salmon, particularly around spawning time. Stale fish are often interested in large flies, irrespective of water height or temperature. Then, they often strike those patterns viciously. To understand this "killer" take, one must remember that even a diminutive salmon parr can fertilize the eggs of an adult female salmon and that, if allowed to do so, this precocious youngster will take part in the mating. Bigger fish therefore, may strike at anything that resembles a parr or threatens their territory.

As elsewhere, the *Rusty Rat* and *Silver Rat* are very popular on Maine rivers. When writing about the *Lady Amherst* I noted its success over the years in the big-fish records of the International Game Fish Association. But starting in 1951, it lost its supremacy to two competitors. The *Rusty Rat* and the *Silver Rat* each hooked the biggest salmon of the year four different times!

Although dedicated seniors still fish them, the classic British patterns now play an insignificant role around the Atlantic. Those with an eye both for tradition and practicality use hair-winged versions extensively; notably the *Thunder & Lightning, Green Highlander, Jock Scott, Blue* or *Silver Doctor*, and the ever-popular *Blue Charm*. Classic color schemes have not been entirely lost, however. For example, the recently mentioned *Wringer* is reminiscent of the *Thunder & Lightning*. Also, the *Rusty Rat* reminds one of the *Jock Scott* and is probably effective because of its similar body-color combinations. The *Black Dose* has also been imitated in numerous simple ways.

While we now prefer simplicity to ostentation, we still appreciate art in craftmanship. We use graphite rods, but we collect the classic split-bamboo models. We insist on efficient reels, but the rare old ones are treasured as museum pieces. Historic or artful flies are collected, protected, and often exhibited, sometimes with tinges of curiosity or envy. The beauty and complexity of the classic salmon fly makes it a perfect candidate for our acquisitive and collecting instincts.

Thus, the return to simplicity in salmon flies does not ordain decline of the classics. On the contrary it marks resurgence in another direction. Growing cults of fly dressers (mainly amateur) emulate and often exceed the old masters in reproducing these historic gems of furs and feathers. Since time is the enemy of the salmon fly, antiques are scarce and usually blemished. They are being replaced by modern dressers to whom precision is paramount and time unimportant. Results prove that fly dressing is a craft that can also be a fine art. Collectors all over the world seek the products of the best dressers. Chapter Fourteen details rebirth of the classic salmon fly as an art.

CHAPTER THIRTEEN

Peregrination

W E who fight the endless battles to preserve our trout and salmon streams may draw strength by reflecting on the story of Iceland, an island not much larger than the state of Maine, where conservation has successfully protected its four score or so rivers for about a thousand years. Of these the snow-fed ones (rather than milky, glacial rivers) of moderate size are most interesting to anglers. In season they teem with salmon.

This steady abundance is due to good management by Icelandic officials, who realize that salmon caught by anglers are worth many times the same number taken commercially. Commercial fishing is allowed only for the excess. Poachers are punished severely. Abutting farmers own the rivers, those on each usually combining to lease rights to middlemen (sometimes Americans) who sell the fishing (usually by the week) to anglers. The price normally includes local transportation and accommodations at comfortable lodges. Each river or section is assigned its quota of rods, thus preventing overfishing and crowding. Sports, attended by their guides, can fish their beats amid rocky gorges or meadow stretches in concentrated solitude, striving for the most effective method or fly. This superb fishing amid awesome scenery is infectious. The only temporary cure is to return, year after year.

On numerous trips to Iceland I have studied flies most popular there, and the whys and whens of their uses. Standard classics remain in vogue: *Blue Charm, Black Doctor, Crosfield, Sweep, Thunder & Lightning, Green Highlander, Jock Scott,* and *Silver Doctor,* more or less in that order of popularity. To these, more modern ones are added, including *Hairy Mary, Francis* (or *Black-Eyed Prawn*), *General*

Practitioner, and tube flies of various sorts including the black one known as *Collie Dog*.

One friend, a mining geologist who has fished for many summers in Iceland, has attempted to hook salmon on each of the 300 patterns given in Kelson's *The Salmon Fly* (1895). Each year he takes along a few dozen classics in various sizes, with spares. So far, he reports success with about half of them.

The Icelanders usually prefer their own patterns, some quite similar to off-island ones. These include *Birna, Blue Sapphire, Eva, Grima, Gryla, Krafla, Porri, Raekja, Skroggur,* and *Tinna*.

Of course we Americans also have our favorites, strangely including the fancy *Night Hawk*, which more simply can be simulated by the *Black Bear* or *Black Rat*. The *Blue, Rusty,* and *Silver Rats* also do well. The *Blue Rat* is a recent pattern conceived in my living room several years ago when a prominent fly dresser asked me what I preferred for Iceland. I mentioned the *Rusty Rat* but said that Icelanders liked "something with blue in it." The *Blue Rat* was the result and is a prime favorite. It is merely the *Rusty Rat* with medium-blue floss substituted for the yellow.

A fly we fish there perhaps more than any other is the *Irish Hairy Mary*, a spin-off of the *Hairy Mary* originated in the early 1960s by John Reidpath, who had a small fishing-tackle shop in Inverness, Scotland. It is one of the first, and probably the best known, of the British hair-wings, so let's look at the original first:

Hairy Mary

Tag Gold tinsel

Tail A topping

Body Black floss (or black wool)

Ribbing Oval gold tinsel

Throat A bright-blue hackle (*Blue Charm* color) tied on as a collar before the wing is applied. (Some dressings call for tying the throat under the hook instead of as a collar.)

Wing A small bunch of reddish-brown fitch tail. (Some dressings call for natural-brown bucktail. In small sizes, brown-barred squirrel tail or hair from the red phase of the squirrel often is used.)

Head Black

Irish anglers brought to Iceland their version of it, called the *Irish Hairy Mary*, in the author's opinion an even better fly. It is the same except that a butt of fluorescent orange floss is added, and the wing is of Irish badger hair. Tag and ribbing usually are silver, but that is a minor matter. It is tied in small sizes, often on double hooks. If I could have only one pattern for Iceland (and the Scandinavian countries) this would be it, but the *Blue Charm* and *Blue* and *Rusty Rats* would be close competitors!

One cannot help but wonder why such a variety of flies are taken by salmon. We only have theories for possible answers. One, fascinating to me, is that some of them simulate elvers in either of two ways. This theory was propounded by Richard Waddington in his revealing but somewhat controversial book *Salmon Fishing* (1948) and was developed by Joseph P. Hubert (the mining geologist recently mentioned) in his *Salmon-Salmon* (1979).

Briefly, it is fact that American and European eels migrate to the Sargasso Sea (northeast of the Bermudas) to mate, their spawn being so great that it fills this part of the sea with glutinous masses. The developing eels drift northward in the Gulf Stream, where, in suitable temperatures, they are presumably intercepted by salmon.

At an early stage the tiny elver (*leptocephalus*) is about the shape and size of a melon seed—iridescent, more or less transparent, and showing eyes and head. If this were envisaged as being mounted on a hook it would be similar in form to a small classic salmon fly.

As these tiny elvers develop and drift farther northward in the Gulf Stream and then in the North Atlantic Current, they elongate to worm shape, providing more substantial food for salmon. This stage is simulated by the *tube fly*. The theory is advanced that salmon, in their home streams, take artificial lures similar to these two stages of eel because their feeding habits are so deeply ingrained in their nature that they will take food even though they do not ingest it to any appreciable extent. Anyway, we know that salmon do take lures simulating leptocephali, so this theory remains interesting, even if not proven as fact.

Tube flies offer a potent weapon in the salmon angler's bag of tricks. Basically they are dressings of hairs or feathers on very short metal or plastic tubes whose bores are only large enough for the leader to pass through. They ride against, or linked to, the hook (usually a treble in Iceland) which is fastened to the leader, thus forming a loose or flexible connection. Loose connections allow the tubes to slide up the leader, out of the way, while a fish is on the hook. Stringing on two or more dressed tubes provides wide varieties of color combinations. We here are concerned only with the flexible connection of the *Collie Dog* tube fly as shown by the accompanying drawing.

Tubes of all sorts can be purchased or made. To dress one, slide an aluminum or brass tube not over half an inch long over an eyeless hook (in a vise) of a size which will hold it snugly. Anchor and cement a few turns of thread around the forward end of the tube; then apply the dressing, such as a three-inch bucktail, leaving enough of the rear end free so a plastic tube can be slipped over it only enough to hold it in place. This type of tube fly has a wing, and possibly a long throat only. It has no body or other dressing.

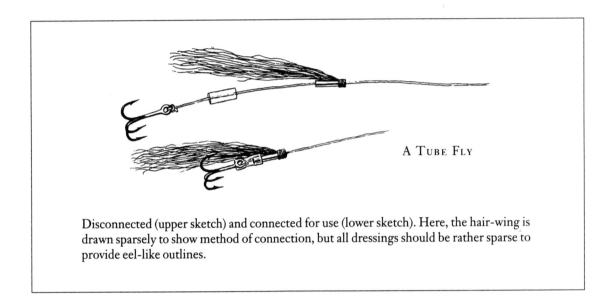

A TUBE FLY

Disconnected (upper sketch) and connected for use (lower sketch). Here, the hair-wing is drawn sparsely to show method of connection, but all dressings should be rather sparse to provide eel-like outlines.

The plastic tube is only long enough to slip snugly over the metal tube at the plastic tube's forward end and to have the hook (tied to the leader) slipped into it at the rear end to form a flexible connection. The hook (usually size 6 or 8 short-shanked straight-eye treble) may need its eye elongated (compressed) a bit with pliers in order to be inserted easily.

The *Collie Dog* is dressed with black thread and the longest black hair of a collie, who shouldn't mind losing a snip or two. The dressing is sparse, just enough to conceal the tubes, and that's all there is to it! I have tried other hair, such as bucktail and bear, with poor results. Fine hair mats and snarls the hook. Stiff hair doesn't fish well. A collie's hair has a texture that seems just right. This "fly," a favorite Iceland pattern, is clearly reminiscent of an immature elver. Could that be why salmon like it so much?

Although authorities say elvers aren't prominent in the salmons' diet, salmon at times hit elver imitations enthusiastically. During this past decade Joe Hubert introduced (in 1977) the Sheep patterns of elver imitations, starting with his *Black Sheep*, so named because it looked so out of place in his boxes of classics.

Black Sheep

Hook: 2 to 6 double (4 is best)

Tag	Fine oval silver tinsel, or wire		and yellow bucktail, mixed, three inches long
Body	Black wool not built up		
Throat	A fairly long and sparse bunch of medium-blue hackle fibers	*Cheeks*	Jungle cock, very short
		Head	Red
Wing	A moderate bunch of black		

Its success inspired a half-dozen or more variations, some with silver or floss bodies and usually darker over a lighter color of bucktail. The very short jungle cock eyes are considered most important in suggesting the prominent eyes of an elver. Note that double hooks are usual. Don't be concerned about the long wing and salmon striking short. If they want the fly, they will have it!

A SHEEP PATTERN

Showing usual configuration of the several variations.

Since salmon attain their pink-red flesh color by feeding on crustaceans such as shrimp (called "prawns" in the British Isles), it follows that flies dressed to imitate them should be effective. One of the very best is Colonel Esmond Drury's *General Practitioner*, which he originated in 1953 and which has been eminently successful ever since. He sent me samples and instructions, which I included in my *Atlantic Salmon Flies & Fishing* (1970), from which the pattern was widely copied. Since that book was published, an angling friend of mine visited the manor house of Mrs. Mary Saunders Davis, who owns both sides of three miles on the (English) River Test. The conversation turned to Colonel Drury and his *General Practitioner*. She said, "He is a dear friend of ours, and the fly was devised right here as a result of my husband's barring Esmond's use of the [preserved] prawn. That creature, as you know, either takes every salmon in the pool or else frightens every fish right out of it. My husband's banning of prawns caused Esmond to create a fly to imitate one, and he came down the next morning with his new and ingenious creation. It proved to be most effective; indeed, almost as deadly as the prawn itself."

Rather than repeat that now-common dressing of the *General Practitioner*, here is another many think is even better. This is the *Black-Eyed Prawn*, often called the *Francis* because it was so named in error in Iceland. It was originated about 1970 by famous fly dresser, Peter Deane, of Sussex, England, who sent me the example shown on Plate XXIII. Its success has brought it international acclaim. Iceland's *Krafla* seems to be a copy of it, using a body of trimmed palmered hackle. The dressing needs a bit of explaining , but this and the illustration should suffice:

Black-Eyed Prawn (or Francis)

Hook: 2 to 8, low-water doubles (occasionally size 0)

Whisks	Six large hackle stalks, stripped of all fibers and tied in so they splay out nearly equidistantly from one another and extend at least three inches long	*Ribbing*	Flat gold tinsel, size 2, or wire
		Hackle	A natural fox-red cock's hackle tied in at stem (*not* point)
Rostrum (nose)	A fairly large bunch of cock pheasant tail fibers set over the whisks and nearly as long as the body	*Body*	Bright-red seal's fur,* thick at hook's bend and tapered to eye, in "carrot-" or cone-fashion
Ribbing floss	One strand, red*	*Eyes*	Two tiny black beads tied in near rear of body, on top, to resemble a pair of eyes
Eye floss	A double strand, red, waxed*	*Head*	Red

The famous *Francis* is dressed in four color combinations, of which the above is the *Red Francis*, which is very popular. The pattern is also done in black, yellow, and dark green, the asterisk calling for these colors then. The green pattern has an "egg-sack" of orange seal's fur applied as a small collar next to the eye of the hook.

Since the dressing is rather unusual, let's review it by steps:

1. Attach the appropriate colored tying thread (according to body color) just short of the eye and wind down in close turns to the bend of the hook.

2. Tie in at the bend the six prepared hackle stalks so they splay out equidistantly. Bind down butts and remove surplus. Take the thread back to bend of hook again.

3. Tie in at least 5 or 6 cock pheasant tail fibers; bind down, cut off surplus, and take the thread again to bend of hook.

4. Tie in one longish strand of ribbing thread of appropriate color.

5. Tie in the ribbing tinsel at exactly the same place.

6. Tie in, again in the same place, a double length of the appropriate colored thread for attaching eyes. (Wire is unsuitable.)

7. Double a fox-red cock's hackle and tie in by the butt at the same place (over bend of hook) as above.

8. Prepare the seal's-fur dubbing; spin on at the bend, and take down the shank just short of the eye. Build up the body into fat carrot shape, tapering to the front.

9. Rib with the tinsel-down body and tie off.

10. Twist the doubled length of eye floss and thread on the two black beads, positioning them as eyes at top of body; then figure-eight with the doubled floss until both eyes are secure at the top of the body. Rib the rest of the body with the surplus floss and secure it at the eye of the hook.

11. Take the ribbing hackle down the body behind each turn of tinsel. Make sure the hackle fibers are sloping back towards the bend and downwards. Any sticking out at the sides or on top are trimmed off with scissors.

12. Wind the final strand of ribbing floss down the body to make the ribbing hackle secure. Whip-finish, and varnish head in appropriate color.

The presence of nonclassics like the *Francis* in a book about classics suggests the modernization of the salmon fly. They provide the necessary link between an historic past and its recent developments, while answering the logical question "What happened next?" But the modern flies of America and Iceland only bring us partly full-circle. So let's briefly summarize flies which have been developed in the rest of *Salmo salar*'s domain.

The lure of Norwegian salmon fishing is due both to the magnificence of the scenery and to the extraordinary size of the fish. As the aircraft descends over the Norwegian coast the granitelike mountains appear to have been ripped, split, and smashed by violent gargantuan claws to form myriad islands, peninsulas, fjords, lakes, and rivers nestled deeply in rocky gorges whose glistening cliffs often rise vertically a few thousand feet above the rippling waters. On more sloping places, and where trees can cling by root-holds to the rock, the country is densely green with pines, firs, and birches. Above the tree line the mountains are bald and grey except for the greenish tinge of mosses. From these escarpments waterfalls cascade from ledge to ledge, fed by small glaciers and patches of perpetual snow.

Down in the valleys neat farms perch on the hillsides, and small towns color-fully display clusters of buildings whose red, blue, yellow, and white roofs protect those making their living from the sea's bounty. In every valley there is a stream, many harboring salmon, flowing through lush countryside where verdant fields are dotted with cattle and sheep. The fields, green with grasses and gardens, are colored in blues, yellows, and pinks by bluebells, clover, buttercups, and thistle. One feels a pervasive peace, quiet, and neatness. There is no litter because the careful always pick up whatever the careless have thrown away.

Comfortable lodges greet anglers, in view of rivers holding salmon as big as fifty pounds or more. But caution should be used in bookings because many rivers are deep, wide, and swift, more suitable to the prawn or wobbling spoon than to the fly. Even on these, however, fly-fishing can provide the ultimate in thrills in quieter stretches of thinner water such as the tails of pools. Smaller streams are more amenable still.

On some rivers all fishing is done at night, under the midnight sun, and from a boat, because wading or casting from shore is impractical. Ghillies are often rather dogmatic about tackle and methods and sometimes profess superiority by denigrating everything in a sport's bounteous and efficient fly books. Finally and grudgingly a ghillie might admit that something like a number-four *March Brown* might do. Listen courteously for you might learn something, and then tactfully use your own judgment. All salmon usually abide by universal ground rules, even though their rules may appear ambiguous to us.

Norwegian ghillies often insist on flies about 3/0 in size on double hooks, but such large ones won't cast comfortably on rods shorter than nine feet. Thus, a ten-footer, or even longer, may be advisable. Even on the big rivers, however, fly sizes 2 or 4 should do well. The ghillies may want to trim them down, and to avoid this a few large low-water patterns may come in handy.

Traditional classics such as *Thunder & Lightning, Lady Amherst, Green Highlander, Durham Ranger,* and *Silver Grey* still are popular, but they are giving way to hair-wings such as *Black Rat, Silver Rat, Rusty Rat, Red Abbey,* and *Cosseboom.* We remember that in Iceland patterns containing blue are popular, but in Scandinavian countries it is somewhat the opposite. The original *Muddler Minnow* is often a happy choice.

The native flies of Norway, such as *Namsen, Ola, Ottesen, Peer Gynt,* and *Sheriff* could be likened to simplified classics. As illustrations, the following two should suffice, originated in the 1960s by John Sand, one of Norway's most famous fly dressers. Sizes most used are 1 and 1/0, with size 6 for sea trout.

Peer Gynt

Tag	Round silver tinsel and yellow floss		*Throat*	Spotted guinea fowl
Tail	A topping and a few short crimson hackle fibers		*Wing*	Two strips of brown mottled turkey, with bronze mallard over it, and a topping
Butt	Black ostrich herl		*Cheeks*	Jungle cock, half as long as the wing
Body	Flat silver tinsel			
Ribbing	Oval silver tinsel		*Horns*	Blue and yellow macaw
Hackle	A crimson hackle from second turn of tinsel		*Head*	Black

Sheriff

Tag	Fine oval gold tinsel			fibers
Tail	A topping, over which are three or four shorter speckled guinea fowl hackle fibers		*Wing*	Two strips of dark turkey tail, with broad strips of bronzed mallard on each side, and a topping
Butt	Black ostrich herl		*Cheeks*	Jungle cock, half as long as the wing
Body	Rear half, flat gold tinsel; front half, black ostrich herl			
Ribbing	Oval gold tinsel		*Horns*	Blue and yellow macaw
Hackle	A yellow hackle, over herl only		*Head*	Black
Throat	Speckled guinea fowl hackle			

Fly tiers who don't want to go to the trouble of dressing complicated shrimp patterns such as the *General Practitioner* and *Black-Eyed Prawn* (or *Francis*) might do as well with this very simple Swedish one called:

———————————————— *Chilimps* ————————————————

Tail The tip of a hot-orange hackle, upright
Body Blood-red wool, fairly thick, and tapered
Ribbing Flat gold tinsel
Hackle A hot-orange hackle leading

the tinsel, with two or three large hot-orange hackles tied in heavily as a collar at the head of the fly and tied back slightly. (There is no wing.)

Head Black

This one, of 1942 vintage, got its name from a black boy in London who was selling shrimp but who mispronounced the word as "chilimps." It is tied in many versions in Scandinavia, one being the *Silver Shrimp*, which is the same except that the rear half of the body is silver tinsel.

Finland, separated in part by the rocky, swift River Tana, or Teno, is reputed to offer the greatest Atlantic salmon fishing bargain in the world. Finland has a border with Norway, and its salmon flies are similar to Norwegian patterns, except that they are very sparsely tied. If visitors prefer American or British patterns, the Finnish Lapps might take scissors and trim them almost to nymph sparseness. Locally tied Teno flies are unique, beautiful, and perfect swimmers, with slender wings and sparse hackles for correct balance.

The salmon flies of France merit scant mention in a book about classics. After the French Revolution the Republic abolished hereditary rights to salmon streams and opened them to all comers. It was a policy guaranteed to encourage the "grab it while you can get it, and to hell with the future" syndrome all too common in other regions. Excessive catches were rampant. The rivers were neglected. Damming for mills (with no bypasses for salmon) and pollution also brought on drastic decline. Netting at sea and along the coasts often blockaded the rivers themselves.

I asked an expert why this was allowed to happen in France. He smiled rather sadly and wryly commented, "Well, I am afraid the Atlantic salmon and the Frenchman are incompatible species."

This grim and too-brief résumé can be concluded by offering a ray of hope currently provided by the growing strength and dedication in France of non-government organizations such as angling groups and nature-protection associations fighting uphill battles to reverse the salmon's decline. Neglect of the fish may account, however, for the simplicity of most French salmon patterns. They are utilitarian, with little consideration for esthetic appeal. One example of the patterns popular in Brittany should suffice:

Bretonne No. 2

Body	Dark-green floss or wool, not built up	*Ribbing*	Fine flat gold tinsel
Hackle	A brown hackle over entire body	*Wing*	Very dark bronze mallard strips

Normandy's patterns verge on the classical: hair-wings adapted from patterns such as *Lemon Grey, Black Doctor, Black Dose, Kate, Silver Grey, Thunder & Lightning, Fiery Brown,* and *Dusty Miller* in sizes usually between 1/o and 4 but in early season as big as 6/o and in low water as small as size 12.

Pyrenéan patterns differ only slightly from standard French ones, local versions being preferred to adaptations of the British classics. A constant feature is the wing of badger hair and/or strips of mallard flank feathers. Bodies are somewhat fuzzy rather than sleek and are made with such substances as seal's fur or boar's wool, usually in colors such as natural, yellow, green, or brown.

Spain's salmon rivers meet the sea at its northwestern coast on the Bay of Biscay. The fifty or so formerly abundant with salmon now are reduced to less than a dozen, of which the Eo, Navia, Narcea, Sella, Deva–Cares, and Ason are prominent. At best, Spain's salmon fishery is a shadow of what it was. The causes of its drastic decline are similar to those of France. In 1936, when Spain was involved in its Civil War, all protections of the salmon were withdrawn and, by the end of the war, when General Franco came into power, whatever was left of the fishery was in desperate straits.

Fortunately General Franco was a salmon fisherman who loved the sport intensely. In 1942 he caused laws to be passed designed to reverse further deterioration. Among these were laws requiring the banning of netting, confining fishing to rods, inaugurating an intensive restocking program, improving the rivers, mandating long prison sentences for poachers, and registering and tagging of salmon. Later steps in this direction also show progress.

Classic patterns of flies such as *Jock Scott, Green Highlander, Dusty Miller, Silver Wilkinson,* and so forth, which still are popular to an extent, are giving way in Spain to simple hair-wings, or hair-wing versions of the classics. Some Spanish anglers use flies as large as from 5/0 to size 2, with smaller ones as the rivers recede and the season advances. Others rarely go above size 2, with sizes 6 or 8 a good average.

We must not conclude this brief mention of fly-fishing in Spain without a few words of praise for its best-known classic fly dresser, Belarmino Martinez, of Pravia, Asturias. Belarmino is a professional devoted to the classics and so expert in dressing even the most complicated patterns that examples of his work are eagerly sought by collectors everywhere. He specializes in innovations of his own design, three of which are illustrated on Plate XXIII. An example is his:

──────────────── *Martinez Special* ────────────────

Tag Fine gold wire and yellow floss
Tail A topping, over which are two very small jungle cock tips, vertical and back to back
Butt Bright-red wool, quite small
Body Rear three quarters, flat gold tinsel; front quarter, pale greenish-yellow chenille
Ribbing Oval gold tinsel, over all
Throat Two or three turns of claret hackle, forward of which is a natural guinea fowl hackle, both pulled down and tied

Wing A pair of tippets, outside of which are married strips of yellow, red, and green swan, outside of which are wide married strips of dark-barred teal and bronze mallard, and one or two toppings
Horns Blue macaw
Sides Jungle cock
Cheeks Kingfisher
Head Black

From the northeastern United States and maritime Canada, through Iceland, the British Isles, the Scandinavian countries, and southward to Spain we have, in the limited space allowed, traced the peregrinations of Atlantic salmon and the flies used to entice them during the nearly 500-year history of sport fishing.

We have seen these flies evolve from the crude to the simple to the extremely elaborate, and back to the simple again.

In no other artificials designed to tempt fish do we see the beauty and complexity found in the classic Atlantic salmon fly. In part a folk art, it can become, in talented and painstaking hands, a truly fine art. So, having noted the decline of the classic salmon fly for fishing, we view in the final chapter the rebirth of it as an art—the crowning challenge to the fly dresser. We must remember that when the classics were originally designed, they were conceived more for the viewing pleasure of the angler than to test the reactions of the salmon. Small matter! We anglers owe a great debt of gratitude to the pioneers who made them possible.

We also owe a debt to the salmon. Are we not, after all, killing the goose which laid the golden egg? Ideally, the Atlantic salmon should be internationally regarded as a sport fish, allowed to roam undisturbed in its pastures of the sea and then to return to its own rivers, full grown, fat, sassy, and clothed in shining silver to challenge anglers with fly rod and fly. Properly managed, salmon can remain in ample supply for sportsmen and commercial fishermen alike. Clearly this is a case when the welfare of the salmon and the requirements of the sportsmen must prevail over human avarice. Dissenters from this viewpoint must be made to realize that salmon taken on fly are worth to local economies many, many times what the same fish are worth when captured by commercial means. Purely stated, death by net or spear is as undeserving for the King of Fishes as it is a costly misfeasance for us.

CHAPTER FOURTEEN

Glorification

RELUCTANTLY or not, we must conclude that the extravagant classic Atlantic salmon fly was conceived by misconception, a product of useless opulence that could not endure as a practical fishing tool. The demand for it was based on the assumption that the more expensive the ingredients and the more lavish the garnishing, the better the fly. The progression to simple patterns indicates that the salmon couldn't care less. The classic flies became popular not only because they were customary but also because they titillated anglers, who considered it a matter of prestige to own and use them.

The majority of the more ornate patterns were devised during the last quarter of the last century—the Victorian era, when extravagance abounded. They were mainly the product of ignorance and lack of scientific knowledge. Kelson, who began writing for the *Fishing Gazette* in 1884 and came to be regarded as the oracle on matters pertaining to salmon flies, had a great deal to do with this. From his writings (although less so in his book) it seems that he actually believed that, in fresh water, salmon fed on various highly localized species of butterflies, and there seems to be no doubt that this belief influenced his whole outlook on salmon flies.

Modern writers, many of whom can't believe that classic flies were made to imitate butterflies, have only to view the high mixed-wing patterns which Kelson advocated, with their butterflylike appendages including horns (antennae). The obvious conclusion has to be "what else?" (See Plates XIV and XV).

The extraordinary fact is not that Kelson held these beliefs, but that succeeding generations of salmon fly-fishermen have apparently accepted these products of ignorance and misconception without question and, perhaps with a bit of perplexity, continued to do so for several subsequent decades. If there was perplexity, it was assuaged by the fact that the flies did take fish.

Kelson must have had a reason for this tenuous belief. In his egotism he may have been jealous of Halford's attainments in chalk stream techniques and, lacking Halford's scientific background and powers of observation, sought to put salmon fishing on the same erudite plane. In his ignorance Kelson became a slave to ornate extravagance, his artistic sense being a reflection of the age.

We can thank Kelson and his associates, however, for their unintended gift to posterity. Common sense dictated the decline of the classic salmon fly for fishing. In turn, we have come to appreciate it as an art form and now celebrate its rejuvenation and glorification, a development promising indefinite life.

Although modern use of the classic salmon fly is confined to a small core of nostalgic anglers, its magnificence and honorable history are far too fascinating to consign it to obscurity. A growing number of fly tiers, always interested in new challenges and techniques, are finding in classic patterns a test of ability and a reward of beauty transcending those afforded by any other form of fly dressing. This art, be it folk or fine, is so absorbing as to become an obsession. For many it provides a never-ending quest toward perfection. What some dressers can do, as color plates herein demonstrate, is nothing short of astounding. I submit that, in the hands of experts, the classic salmon fly becomes a new form of fine art!

As an art form, the salmon fly attracts a new cult of collectors who specialize in acquiring fine or historic examples. Some are expert fly dressers themselves and collect partly to compare their work to that of others. Others, like myself, do it as a fascinating hobby, one that, like coin collecting, requires little storage room and display space.

Like dressing the classics, collecting can begin simply and be carried as far as one wishes. My fascination with it began with my love and respect for salmon fishing. I studied and experimented with the various angling techniques, which of course required delving into books—all leading to growing familiarity with the various styles and characters of salmon flies. This led to a fascination with the flies themselves.

At first I collected them to have a supply of the various patterns for fishing. At that early time classics were still in vogue, and I favored them because of their beauty. I learned to respect them because of their old and often debatable histories highlighted in such books as Reverend Henry Newland's *The Erne: Its Legends and Its Fly Fishing* (1851). I submit that one cannot appreciate the full flavor of tying or collecting classics without studying books about them. Those mentioned in this text are listed in the bibliography. Wisely selected, such books provide a lifetime of pleasure as well as a good investment.

Fishing trips around the northern Atlantic put me in touch with fly dressers, tackle shops, and beneficiaries of estates who had old classics to sell or barter. I acquired too many, forcing later cullings. I say "too many" because these old flies were nearly always commercial efforts which, because they were produced for trade, lacked precision. Aged flies also usually are mussed and often faded. Mussing can be helped by steaming, but collectors should learn to be selective. "Antiques" are proper in any collection, especially if they can be traced to famous sources, but there are also better choices, as we shall see. Since these old flies usually are mussed, they need intelligent preening. Careful attention can do wonders in making many presentable.

After such restoration, both old flies and contemporary patterns require protection and identification. My solution to this is to mount individuals on stiff, white cards about 3¾ by 2⅛ inches to fit transparent envelopes. Printing firms can supply both. Hold the fly on the card by sewing it in place with thread. Transparent adhesive tape can also be used, although it may affect the finish of hooks in long storage. First, however, print the name of the fly on the bottom face of the card and write pertinent information about it on its back.

Thus each fly is individually mounted and sealed so it can be filed or viewed without mussing. Moth eggs can be a problem although this method minimizes them. If there is any suspicion of moths or other parasites, the fly should be quarantined with moth repellent for a few weeks before mounting. Mounted flies can be filed alphabetically in boxes made to accommodate them.

Collectors who wish to display certain flies can do so in various ways. I had some framed by a professional who mounted each by attaching it with supposedly water-soluble adhesive to a tacklike transparent peg sealed into a drilled hole in the background. This affords a very attractive framing, but it remains to be seen whether the "water-soluble" adhesive can be entirely soaked off. I doubt it. Perhaps a better way is to sew the fly to its background with fine thread or monofilament. Then the fly can be easily removed and completely restored by steaming. Another way is to merely lay flies under a glass-topped exhibition table. Mounting individuals impaled by their hook points to small pieces of cork or driftwood glued to the wooden bases of glass globes also provides a pleasing effect.

One should have a plan for collecting. For example, my collection started with specializing in the 300 or so patterns given in Kelson. Bearing in mind that dressings in some books do not always entirely agree with those in others, identification of pattern sources is important.

Collectors find that common classics like *Jock Scott*, *Green Highlander*, and so forth prevail, and that old examples of exotic patterns are nearly nonexistent. Beyond selecting a classic for workmanship and condition, remember that a fly is more valuable if it contains the correct feathers, such as real Indian crow rather than a substitute. Hard-to-find patterns can be supplied by contemporary tiers. The best of their work is far superior to most of the older examples. Collectors soon learn who the true experts are, and who is on the way up. As in the world of painting, some of these artists are famous or will become so: therefore duplicate patterns by promising dressers can increase a collection's value and interest.

I feel it is a mistake for collectors to disparage contemporary patterns as "reproductions." All classics are reproductions except the originals. For example, the only original *Jock Scotts* are the ones dressed by Jock himself. All others are copies, or duplicates, distinguished only by age, quality, and the persons who dressed them. I would rather have a *Jock Scott* modernly dressed by an expert like Alcott, Cohen, or Fabbeni than one made by one of Jock's contemporaries. Comparisons of the old to the new indicate that the best of the new dressers do better work! Study, for example, the patterns dressed by Albert J. Cohen on Plate XV. He took more than ten hours to dress each of these flies. How many of the old-time tiers would put such care and precision into their work?

Those interested in learning to dress the classics should not be discouraged by the complexities. Any fly tier with basic knowledge can start with simple ones (such as given in Chapters Nine and Ten) and proceed from there. If the art lacked difficulty, it would also lack the challenge that makes it so satisfying.

I notice that the very best classic dressers are people who study the art by referring to the classic authors such as Pryce–Tannatt, Hale, and Kelson. So do your homework, and always continue it. Books such as those listed in the bibliography are easiest to obtain from dealers in out-of-print angling books, some of whom advertise in fly-fishing magazines. Purchased prudently, even at high prices, they tend to increase in value. Studying them affords incomparable knowledge of this hobby's scope as well as providing authentic dressing instruction. Experts would advise the less accomplished to alternately study and practice.

If you take up fly dressing yourself, you will soon reach a point where personal help is needed to solve one difficulty or another. Find an *able* teacher, and don't settle for second rate! Many points, difficult to master from texts, become easy following personal instruction. Start simply and build ability gradually. Use iron-eyed hooks at first, but remember that gut-eyed ones are proper for the classics because they were in vogue during Victorian times. Don't worry about using proper feathers. Practice with substitutes or anything else that appears logical. Practice leads to perfection! Never plead lack of ability. Experts come from all walks of life.

One man who many think has reached the goal of perfection in classic fly dressing (but who denies attaining it) is a big person with large hands who lacks higher education. If old masters, like those just mentioned, could view the results of his efforts I'm sure they would be astounded. He is someone who has come as close to perfection as human hands can attain. The color plates in this book illustrate his skill as well as that of others. His name is Ronald K. Alcott, of Groton, Massachusetts. He provided the following comments.

Alcott credits his original interest in the classics to reading my book *Atlantic Salmon Flies & Fishing* and studying the color plates therein, but that book mainly discusses salmon fishing and salmon-fly patterns, not fly tying. He says he began differentiating between feathers of individual birds, even those of the same species. "Similar feathers may look alike, but they are not, " he says. "There are great differences in suitability and quality." The following three paragraphs are from his notes to me:

> The next problem (even more significant) is differences in *techniques*. How can one possibly copy an old master's work if that person does not tie with exactly the same technique as used in the fly being copied?
>
> After much trial and error I realized that just looking at pictures wasn't the way to learn. I was going to have to *read and study*, so I bought all the suitable books I could find and read them over and over; each time learning something new. Each book gave a different opinion of how a classic fly should be dressed, so I selected advice and formed my own methods. But, if I am tying a specific fly whose pattern is given in a book, I follow that pattern exactly, and so label it. Avoid hybrids!
>
> Study *proportions*. Most flies have shortcomings in this respect. One of the best color plates to study for correct proportions is the first one in *Salmon Fishing* (1948) by Eric Taverner. The next factor is *self-discipline*. Establish a technique and system of material selection that leads to the goal of perfection, and don't change it unless shown a better one. The hardest lesson I had to learn was to stop and redo an imperfect step, or to discard a fly and start over.

Ronald Alcott sums up this advice by repeating that there are no substitutes for *study* and *practice*.

When one reaches the stages at which fly dressing can be called an art rather

A CLASSIC SALMON FLY DRESSER AT HIS BENCH

Ronald K. Alcott, of Groton, Massachusetts

than merely a craft, one might take added pleasure in dressing exhibition patterns, as illustrated on several of these color plates and particularly on Plate XXIV. Exhibition patterns, of course, can be superior dressings of standard patterns, but they also can be new ones conceived in honor of a person or event. In these, artists go all-out to do their very best work both in ability and in authentic material selection.

If such flies are standard patterns, such as Ronald Alcott's *Jock Scott* shown on Plate XIX, ingredients are limited to those which could have been used in the mid-1800s or whenever the pattern was originated. This rules out the practice of using ingredients developed or discovered since then, such as substituting monofilament for silkworm gut for eye loops. Period hooks, which can frequently be reclaimed from damaged old flies, are preferred to modern hooks.

Exhibition patterns favor following specific dressings, preferably without variation, as given in old books. Most important, they call for the finest work of their dressers. They are intended to be the peak of the art in modern salmon-fly dressing!

Many practitioners of this art favor following established patterns rather than originating new ones. The former usually are the more valuable, but there is nothing to prevent exhibiting one's own ingenuity, and the results can be very handsome, as some of the flies on Plate XXIV show. If such "vanity patterns" are named for, and presented to, specific individuals, they make gifts that are far more cherished than "store-bought" objects of even greater value.

This book marks a lifetime study of, and appreciation for, classic salmon flies. Its author is old enough to have observed their decline in favor of simpler and more practical patterns. While their decline was viewed with regret, it is a joy to see the cherished classics blossom out in new forms. This gradual movement back to the classic patterns has burst into a challenging art form practiced by rapidly growing numbers of enthusiastic adherents from every walk of life.

The author hopes that those who peruse or study this book will appreciate why this craft can, in its highest form, be considered a true art. It is my hope that many more will follow in the footsteps of the practitioners whose creations grace these pages.

Fly Dressers Represented

Numbers refer to color plates

Alcott, Ronald K., Groton, Massachusetts
III, XVII, XIX, XXIV

Arnason, Gudmundur, Reykjavik, Iceland
XXIII

Bates, Joseph D., Jr., Longmeadow,
Massachusetts XXI

Bean, Paul R., Sherbrooke, Quebec XX

Bigaouette, Carmelle, Matapedia, Quebec
XXI

Borders, Larry G., USAF VII, XI, XII,
XIII, XVI, XVIII, XIX, XXIV

Boyd, Megan, Brora, Scotland X, XVIII,
XXIV

Cohen, Albert J., Dallas, Texas XIV

Deane, Peter, Sussex, England XXIII

DeFeo, Charles, New York, New York
XXII

Drury, Esmond, Lincolnshire, England
XXIII

Ent, Robert W., Bangor, Maine XXI

Fabbeni, Brian G., Powys, Wales V, X,
XII, XXIV

Gapen, Don, Anoka, Minnesota XXI

Gislasson, Kristjan, Reykjavik, Iceland
XXIII

Glasso, Sydney, Forks, Washington VI, XI,
XVIII

Godfrey, Ted, Reisterstown, Maryland
IX, XII, XV, XVIII, XX, XXIV

Hardy Brothers, Ltd., London, England
XVI

Heddon, Jack, London, England II

Hibbitts, Robert C., Cape Coral, Florida
XVIII

Jorgensen, Poul, Roscoe, New York XIX

Kelson, George M., London, England XV

MacPherson, Maxwell, Bristol,
New Hampshire III, XX

Malloch, Peter D., Perth, Scotland XV, XIX

Martinez, Belarmino, Pravia, Spain XXIII

Miller, Gene, Pleasant Valley, Connecticut XXIII

Mills, William, & Son, New York,
New York XX

Mouches–Ragot, Loudéac, France XXIII

Mustad, O. & Son, Oslo, Norway XXIII

Newcomb, Ronald, Jay, Maine XXI

Niemeyer, Ted, Seattle, Washington XXII

Olsen, Olaf, Laerdal, Norway XXIII

Sand, Erling, Engerdal, Norway XXIII

Simpson, Alex, Aberdeen, Scotland III, IV

Veverka, Robert, Underhill, Vermont XI

Waslick, Mark W., Middlebury, Vermont
XV

Westfall, Claude Z., Orono, Maine XXI

Younger, Jimmy, Dumfries, Scotland XVIII

Bibliography
of books and periodicals quoted or mentioned

Adamson, Dr. W. A., *see* Alexander, Col. J. E.

Aldam, W. H., *Flees, and the Art a Artyfichall Flee Making*, London, 1875.

Alexander, Col. J. E. (Editor), *Salmon Fishing in Canada*, London, 1860. Also simultaneous, Putnam, N.Y.

(Anon.), *The North Country Angler*, London, 1786.

Bainbridge, George C., *The Fly Fisher's Guide*, Liverpool, 1816. And other editions.

Barker, Thomas, *The Art of Angling*, London, 1651. And other editions.

Barnes, Dame Julyans, *see* Berners, Dame Juliana.

Bates, Col. Joseph D., Jr., *Atlantic Salmon Flies & Fishing*, Harrisburg, Pa., 1970.

Belton, —, *The Angler in Ireland*, London, 1834.

Berners, Dame Juliana, *The Boke of St. Albans*, St. Albans, 1486. And other editions.

Blacker, William, *Art of Angling*, London, 1842.

Blacker, William, *Blacker's Art of Fly Making*, London, 1855.

Bowlker, Richard and Charles, *The Art of Angling* by Richard Bowlker, Worcester, England, 1747. Second edition, 1774 and all later editions by Charles Bowlker.

Brookes, Richard, *The Art of Angling*, London, 1766. And other editions.

Chaytor, A. H., *Letters to a Salmon Fisher's Sons*, London, 1910.

Chitty, Edward, *see* Theophilus South (pseud.).

Cooper & Forshaw, *The Birds of Paradise and Bower Birds*, Boston, 1977

Ephemera (pseud.). See Fitzgibbon, Edward.

Ettingsall, Thomas, *The Green Bank* (a rhymed angling treatise including an excellent list of Irish flies), Dublin, 1850.

Fitzgibbon, Edward, *Book of the Salmon*, London, 1850.

Francis, Francis, *A Book on Angling*, London, 1867. And other editions.

Franck, Richard, *Northern Memoirs*, London, 1694.

H. (R.), *The Angler's Sure Guide*, Little-Brittain, 1706. (Generally attributed to Robert Howlett.)

Hale, J. H., *How to Tie Salmon Flies*, London, 1892. And other editions.

Hansard, George A., *Trout and Salmon Fishing in Wales*, London, 1834.

Hardy, Campbell, *Forest Life in Acadie*, London, 1869. And other editions.

Hardy, John, *Salmon Fishing*, London, 1907.

Henderson, William, *My Life as an Angler*, London, 1876.

Hubert, Joseph P., *Salmon-Salmon*, privately printed in an edition of 100 copies, 1979.

Kelson, George M., *The Salmon Fly*, London, 1895. And an American reprint, 1979.

Kirkbride, John, *The Northern Angler*, London, 1837.

Knox, A. E., *Autumns on the Spey*, London, 1872.

Markham, Gervaise, *The English Husbandman*, London, 1614. And other editions.

Mascall, Leonard, *A Book of Fishing with Hooke and Line*, London, 1590. And other editions.

Maxwell, Sir Herbert, *Salmon and Sea Trout*, London, 1898.

McDonald, John, *The Origins of Angling*, New York, 1963.

Newland, Rev. Henry, *The Erne, Its Legends and Its Fly Fishing*, London, 1851.

Norris, Thaddeus, *American Angler's Book*, Philadelphia, 1864. And other editions.

O'Gorman, —, *The Practice of Angling*, Dublin, 1845 and 1855.

Phair, Charles, *Atlantic Salmon Fishing*, New York, 1937.

Pryce–Tannatt, Dr. Thomas E., *How to Dress Salmon Flies*, London, 1914. And a later edition.

Roosevelt, Robert B., *The Game Fish of the North*, New York, 1884. And other editions.

Russell, Jack, *Jill and I and the Salmon*, Boston, 1950.

Sage, Dean, *The Ristigouche and Its Salmon Fishing*, Edinburgh, 1888. And a 1973 American edition.

Scott, Jock (Donald Rudd), *Greased Line Fishing for Salmon*, London, 1937. And other editions.

Scrope, William, *Days and Nights of Salmon Fishing on the Tweed*, London, 1843. And other editions.

Snow, David, *The Cotingas*, Ithaca, N. Y., 1982.

South, Theophilus (Edward Chitty), *The Fly Fisher's Text Book*, London, 1841.

Stoddart, Thomas T., *The Angler's Companion*, Edinburgh and London, 1847. Other editions 1853 and 1864.

Taverner, Eric, *Fly Tying for Salmon*, Edinburgh, 1942.

Taverner, Eric, *Salmon Fishing*, London, 1948.

Taylor, Samuel, *Angling in All its Branches*, London, 1800.

Venables, Robert, *The Experienced Angler*, London, 1662. And other editions.

Wade, Henry, *Halcyon*, London, 1861.

Walton, Izaak, *The Universal Angler*, London, 1676. (Including Charles Cotton and Robert Venables.) And other editions.

Younger, John, *River Angling*, Edinburgh, 1840. And other editions

PERIODICALS

The American Fly Fisher, Vol. 4, No. 3, 1982 (Hoffman).

The Field (newspaper), February 18, 1893 ("Punt Gun"), and other issues.

Forest and Stream, August 12, 1880 (H. L. Leonard).

Salmon and Trout, January 7, 1923 (Ernest Crosfield).

Sports Illustrated, May 27, 1957 (McDonald and Webster).

Wildwood's Magazine, 1888 (Daniel Webster).

Index

The names of flies are printed in *italic*; roman numerals following these names refer to the color plate in which the fly is shown. Titles of books are printed in CAPITALS AND SMALL CAPITALS.